Historic MOVIE THEATRES OF NEW MEXICO

Historic MOVIE THEATRES OF NEW MEXICO

JEFF BERG

THE History PRESS

Published by The History Press
Charleston, SC
www.historypress.com

First published 2018

Manufactured in the United States

ISBN 9781467137799

Library of Congress Control Number: 2018936091

CONTENTS

PREFACE

I do, sort of, remember the first movie that I ever saw in a real genuine movie theatre. I was in grade school, perhaps third or fourth grade, and I went to the Catlow Theater in my (very) old hometown of Barrington, Illinois.

I went with one of my best friends of the time, Steve Willard, whose father owned several fast-food emporiums called Dog n' Suds. Steve, a slightly nervous lad, was nonetheless a good pal and claimed to have "invented" the cheese dog, something he ate frequently, by glopping Cheez Whiz on a hot dog and downing it in a few quick bites. Yum.

We were accompanied by his annoyed sister, whose name I think was Kathy. I always remember her, since her room at Steve's house always had any number of half-empty or half-full glasses of Coca-Cola or souring milk scattered about. Steve's mom was into Siamese cats—the house had a number of same, none of which had any boundaries—and they slept, jumped, yowled and did other cat things as they pleased. I recall a birthday cake at Steve's house that had more cat hair than icing. Nevertheless, Kathy had begrudgingly agreed to haul us with her when she and some girlfriend went to the "picture show."

Sadly, I don't remember which Jerry Lewis movie it was—perhaps it was *The Bellboy* (1960). Doesn't matter. But the theatre was so crowded that I remember having to sit in the aisle (take that, fire marshal!) with Steve and some other soon-to-be-wayward youth. The audience howled at the picture, and I probably did at times as well, but I recall being *much* more interested in the theatre and the atmosphere created by the audience.

The Catlow, at this writing, still exists and is still independent and has been since opening in 1927. It mostly runs popular features where patrons can vote for the next feature, and the lobby is now connected to a popular sandwich shop next door. I find that interesting because I nearly purchased a theatre and sandwich shop myself in the early 1990s in Estancia, New Mexico. May it rest in peace.

The Catlow wasn't enormous, but it was comfy and roomy. The seats were of red velvet or velveteen, and there were tiny faux box seat balconies on either side of the screen at an angle. There was also a small clock on the left side near the balcony, outlined in blue neon. I always thought that was a good idea. The clock is gone now, but most everything else, updated and ashine, is the same about the Catlow.

The audience was in fine form, ready for a laugh—many laughs, since this was probably the prime of Jerry Lewis's movie career. I attended the Catlow many more times over the years, and when I must—and I do mean *must*—return to Illinois, I always try to go for a screening at the theatre, which still has an outdoor marquee that looks the same as it did those years ago.

I also attended movies in many of the ornate and long-gone theatres of downtown Chicago—State-Lake (about 2,500 seats), the Chicago, the McVickers (which did Cinerama), Woods, United Artists, Loop and the Marina Cinemas, which was the first place I ever saw a movie as one of two audience members, my girlfriend being the other, when we watched *Walkabout*, which is one of my favorite films of all time.

Since leaving Illinois, I've been to countless theatres, having lived in Wyoming, Montana, Alaska, Colorado and California, until alighting in New Mexico (for the third time). I've worked at theatres—as a volunteer and later a board member and special events planner for the Fountain Theatre, in Mesilla, New Mexico, which you will read more about in this book, as well as at the Jean Cocteau Cinema in Santa Fe, owned by famed author George R.R. Martin, as assistant manager of that venue.

This book will concentrate on old movie theatres of New Mexico, most of which are gone now, but in special cases, I have included theatres that are still operating. I will tell you tidbits about their histories, their fates and their lifespans. It seems that almost every town in New Mexico once had a movie theatre, and in some cases a movie palace, that served the populace well for many years. Do note that I am not able to cover every old theatre in the state—perhaps this will lead to Volume 2. Some research offered hints at theatres that may have existed at one time or another in very small towns, such as Berino, Bluewater, Carthage, Madrid, Columbus and Hachita.

Sadly, movie theatres have taken a back seat to home viewing, with many people even watching movies on their cellphones rather than experiencing the brief, albeit marvelous camaraderie of a theatre filled with fellow moviegoers.

However, the number of theatres is on the rise in the United States. The National Association of Theater Owners (NATO) reported that as of January 2017, there were 39,579 indoor screens and 595 drive-ins, for a total of 40,174. Not bad.

The book is organized in four broad sections, more or less. The southern part of New Mexico is first, due to its interesting history. Connected with that is the southwest portion, followed by the central and southeast. From there, on this dizzying little trip, we head to the rural northeast portion of the state, to the northwest and, finally, end up in the mostly populated areas, Albuquerque and Santa Fe.

I hope you will find this book fun and interesting and one that you can gain a lot of knowledge from as well.

And now for our main feature…

ACKNOWLEDGEMENTS

This book is dedicated to Marty the cat, whose fierce and loving spirit changed my life. My heartfelt thanks to the following good folks—Bob Christensen, whom I met online when I asked to use some of his outstanding photos in this work, applying his fifty years of photographing vernacular architecture around New Mexico; Randy Carlisle; for permission to use some of his terrific photos; Robert Yee and Ysabel Velarde, for their photo contributions; and to anyone who has ever gone to a movie with me.

SOUTH-CENTRAL AND SOUTHWEST NEW MEXICO

There seems to be some debate as to who made the first moving picture, which is the best that the concept could be called at the time since early films were generally brief, experimental kinds of works.

Among the contenders are the Lumière brothers of France, who were early pioneers in the motion picture industry. They "screened" several short works, one of which showed workers leaving their factory, as well as other short pieces for which they charged admission at the Salon Indien, located at the Grand Café in Paris. This took place in December 1895. One could think of the café as the first movie theatre.

Thomas Edison was a pioneer of film in the United States, using his invention of the kinetoscope to screen the works of his crews in various places. Edison's production company is credited with shooting the first piece of film shot in New Mexico, "Indian Day School," which is a fifty-second loop of American Indian children entering and leaving the Isleta Pueblo School. It is also of interest historically, as you can observe the attempt to Anglicize the children by cutting their hair and dressing them in contemporary clothes.

It is claimed that the first movie theatre opened in Los Angeles in June 1902. The Electric Theatre, housed in a tent, charged a dime for an hour-long presentation. This followed several years of short films being shown at vaudeville shows and in nickelodeons, with one of the first, ironically called the Nickelodeon, hosting more than four hundred people in Pittsburgh.

Other claims include the Vitascope Hall, located in New Orleans (1896), which is said to be the first permanent movie house in the country. It charged a dime, had two shows a day and accommodated four hundred guests, and for an extra dime, you could get a glimpse into the booth to watch the projectionist operate the Vitascope itself. At present, though, the location is a Burger King. Or maybe the "first" was the Berlin Wintergarten Theater, which showed short films in 1895.

Many of the earliest theatres merely added film to the list of other things they offered—live theatre, concerts and often vaudeville. With this, as noted by sociologist Mae D. Huettig some years later in 1944, by adding silent movies to their repertoire, "exhibitors were unwittingly digging the grave of vaudeville."

By the 1930s, cinemas had become so popular that cultural critic Gilbert Seldes observed that "the success of the early motion picture industry grew from its ability to compel people to leave their homes in anticipation of entertainment [and] to go to any movie rather than not go at all."

We may never know exactly who was first, but in terms of movies being shown, it wasn't long before New Mexico became part of the big picture. Over the years, 222 movie theatres have come and gone (or survive) here in the Land of Enchantment, while at this writing, only 52 operate, most of them as part of one national chain or another.

For a change, it was not Santa Fe or Albuquerque that offered something new or first when it came to picture shows. Rather, it was Mesilla, a small, quaint village attached at the hip to Las Cruces in far south-central New Mexico. (Grant's Opera House in Albuquerque did screen films of Teddy Roosevelt's Rough Riders in 1898. The opera house suffered a large fire the following year.)

The Fountain Theatre opened in 1905 (and remains open and running strong to this day in 2018 thanks to the Mesilla Valley Film Society). It showed "lantern slides," which according to the Magic Lantern Society "had its origins in 17th century and were optical viewing devices which came to be known as 'magic lanterns.' The earliest slides for magic lanterns consisted of hand-painted images on glass, projected by itinerant showmen telling stories about the images that were projected."

There are numerous variations of the lantern slide, some being mechanical and others being stills. The Fountain, which today is considered an "arthouse" cinema, showing movies that contain more story than action, also screened short films.

According to David G. Thomas, the author of *Screen with a Voice*, the Rink Theater, which opened in 1885 as a playhouse and skating rink, also started showing movies in 1907 in Las Cruces. According to Thomas, these were followed by the Vaudette Moving Picture Company, located briefly in the rear of the Ideal Grocery Store, and the Electric Theater, which was placed in the local Armory Building. Both opened in 1908, with the Vaudette lasting only a few months, while the Electric, which changed its name to the Grand and later to the Bijou during a partnership, did enough business to carry on until sometime in 1911. Another source claimed, without mentioning the name of the theatre, that Mansour and Arthur Farah opened the first cinema in Las Cruces.

In case you thought that the drive-in movie theatre started in the 1930s in New Jersey, as is often reported, Thomas's fine book might be able to change that erroneous notion. According to his research, the Wonderland Theater opened as an outdoor venue, seating three hundred and projecting onto a large wall rather than a screen. First called the Airdome, it soon closed and moved to compete with another upstart, the Crystal, the owner of which, Roline Banner, provided stiff competition to the more established theatres in town.

Banner soon opened his own "open-air movie palace," calling it the Open-Air Picture Show. This set the owners of the Airdome, two gents named Bennett and Birdwell, into motion, with the two partners starting work on another cinema, a new Airdome. The unique thing about this undertaking is that besides having a capacity of 450, almost unheard of in 1914, they also had "an automobile drive [that] will hold two rows of cars, 10 in all, permitting the occupants to see the performance without leaving their cars."

A second "drive-in," the Theatre de Guadalupe, with space for forty (or more) cars, opened in 1915, lasting just over a year, which included a name change to the De Luxe after just a few weeks.

An innovative idea, but never patented (hence the 1933 New Jersey claim), it is not clear how long some of these outdoor emporiums lasted, but probably not long, as Las Cruces, in the heart of the Chihuahuan Desert, can be brutally hot in the summer and is often drenched by desert "monsoons"—brief, heavy and often violent thunderstorms that often carry on late in the day in July and August.

By 1912, it is said that Albuquerque, the state's largest city then and now, was just catching on and boasted at least five places that showed "moving pictures," including its own Airdome and Crystal (different owners than those in Las Cruces), the Orpheum, the Pastime and a site called the Elk.

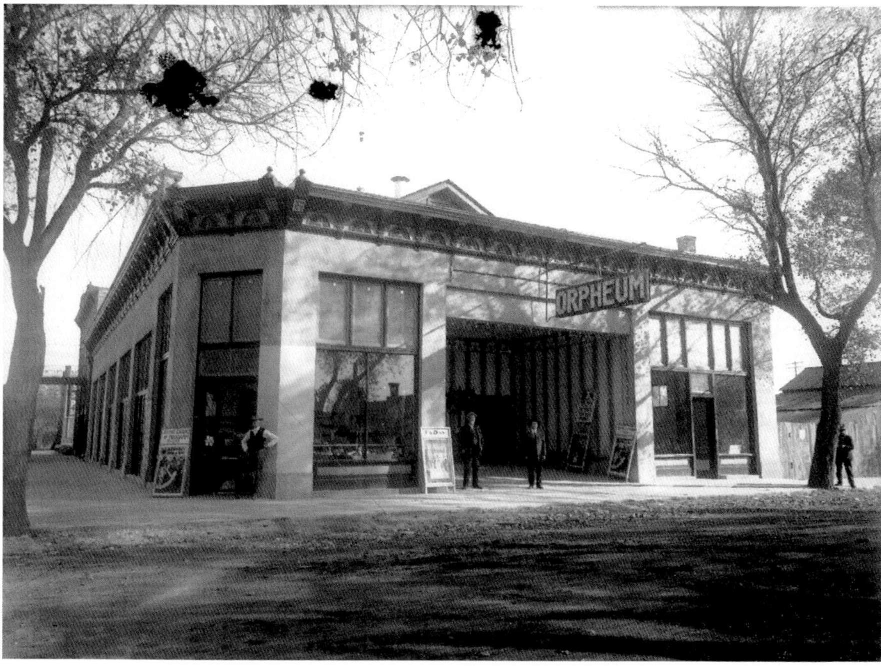

Orpheum Theater, Albuquerque. *Albuquerque History Museum.*

Other theatres in Las Cruces through the years included the Rio Grande, a movie theatre from its opening in 1926, screening the silent film *Mare Nostrum* (*By the Sea* in Latin). Historian David Kammer's research observed that "with the completion of the Rio Grande Theater, the town of Las Cruces had, not only a modern theatre, but a facility that discounted tickets for merchant-sponsored community nights, hosted American Legion benefits, and offered a stage for the town's baby popularity contest."

It thrived for years, finally closing in 1998 with a screening of *U.S. Marshals*, which starred Tommy Lee Jones, who lives near Las Cruces in far west Texas. It went through several owners, but ultimately it fell on hard times. The Allen Theatre Group, which has a monopoly on all the screens in Las Cruces (and several other New Mexico cities), opened a new twin-screen operation immediately after shuttering the Rio.

In 2005, it was reopened as a beautifully restored multiuse center that now mostly hosts small concerts and stage performances. It is now operated by the City of Las Cruces.

The Aggie Drive-In operated from 1966 to 1990, and as did many theatres that were faltering over the years, it turned to adult features, such as *Caged Virgins* and *The Girl in Room 2A*, around 1974. One has to wonder if any theatre in New Mexico ever screened the state's contribution to such fare, *Teenage Seductress*, which was shot in Taos in the 1970s and promptly forgotten. The Aggie later added a screen but was eventually completely torn down. Oddly, upon its opening by a gent named Lamar Gwaltney, the owner of Lamar Liquors Inc. and later a New Mexico state senator, the six-hundred-space drive-in, which had a single ninety- by sixty-foot screen, advertised family entertainment. Its first features were *Charade* and *I'd Rather Be Rich*. A second screen was added in 1982, perhaps to show *Caged Virgins: Part 2*. (Just kidding…I think.)

Las Cruces was festooned with drive-in theatres back in their heyday. The other outdoor screens included the Rocket, which opened in 1952 and closed in 1965, and the Organ Drive-In, named for the nearby Organ Mountains, which resemble a pipe organ in stature.

The Organ was the first, opening in the late summer of 1948, with space for six hundred cars. It even offered attendants who would "take refreshment orders from the car." In 1955, things were faltering, possibly due to outdated equipment, and the theatre was closed for several weeks before reopening as the Fiesta. In 1961, the Fiesta daringly offered adult

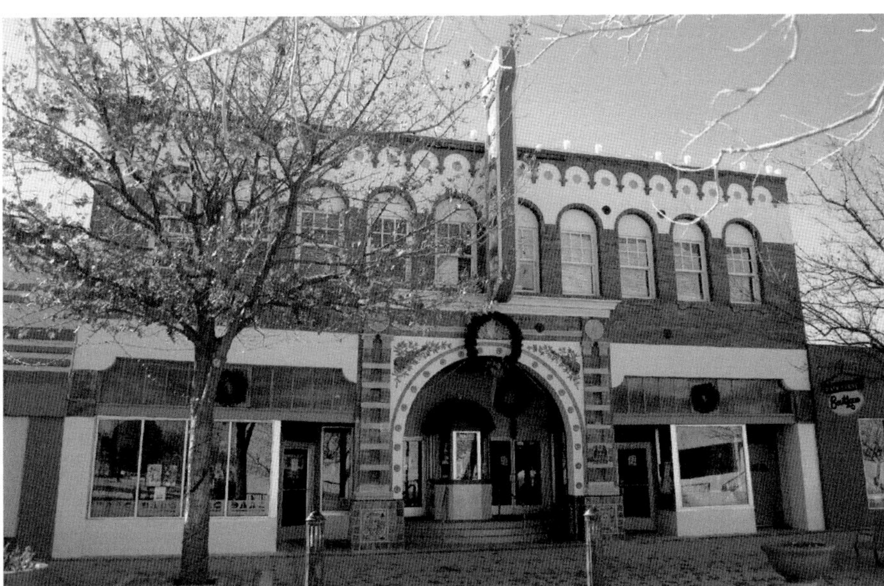

Rio Grande Theatre, Las Cruces (restored). *Randy Carlisle.*

entertainment, such as *Garden of Eden*, which boasted that it had been shot at a "real nudist park." For those in the know, Las Cruces has its own "nudists," although the correct term is "naturist." The folks who enjoy clothing-optional freedom at the Sun Tree Travel Club are, as I was told when I did an article about them some years ago, "doing the same things you are doing, just without clothes."

The Fiesta and the Aggie, the two remaining drive-ins, were purchased by an outfit called Video Independent Theaters, but their fate was that of most drive-ins: the Fiesta, despite its best efforts, closed for good in 1981.

Indoor theatres also had deep competition for some years in Las Cruces. Opening and closing over the years were the State, Mission and Plaza. The State, with two hundred seats, opened just weeks after the United States entered World War II in December 1941. It was always a single-screen house, but it also fell on hard times and closed in 1975. It sat vacant for a few years before becoming the home of the Las Cruces Community Theatre (LCCT). Over the years, the LCCT has faced several challenges, including the condition of the old building and the fact that in early 2016, the property was for sale; it's now off the market, and LCCT thrives.

The Mission Theater was not really in La Cruces but rather in what was then a nearby unincorporated area of Dona Ana County, Mesilla Park. Opening in the spring of 1937, it was built and owned by Rod Bason, a local businessperson.

For the times, it was a step ahead, being air conditioned and "acoustically treated," replete with a lounge and a stage. The Mission, according to *Screen with a Voice*, hosted one of the most unusual events ever offered in movie theatre history when it scheduled a raffle for a six-week-old baby girl in March 1938. Present were a doctor and nurse to "certify" the baby's health (but not so the mental health of the theatre manager, Hershel Wheeler), as well as an attorney and the baby's parents to legalize the adoption papers. No real follow-up seems to exist to this event, other than Wheeler's claim that "if a winner does not want the baby, I shall be glad to have the adoption papers made out to me." (Maybe this is why I like movies so much and never really knew my parents.)

Wheeler also sponsored a football guessing contest in 1937, with "two passes to each of the amateur prophets predicting the highest number of games correctly." This is rather unclear, is it not?

The theatre changed hands several times in the 1930s and 1940s, finally faltering and closing for good after a new name change to the Park in April 1962.

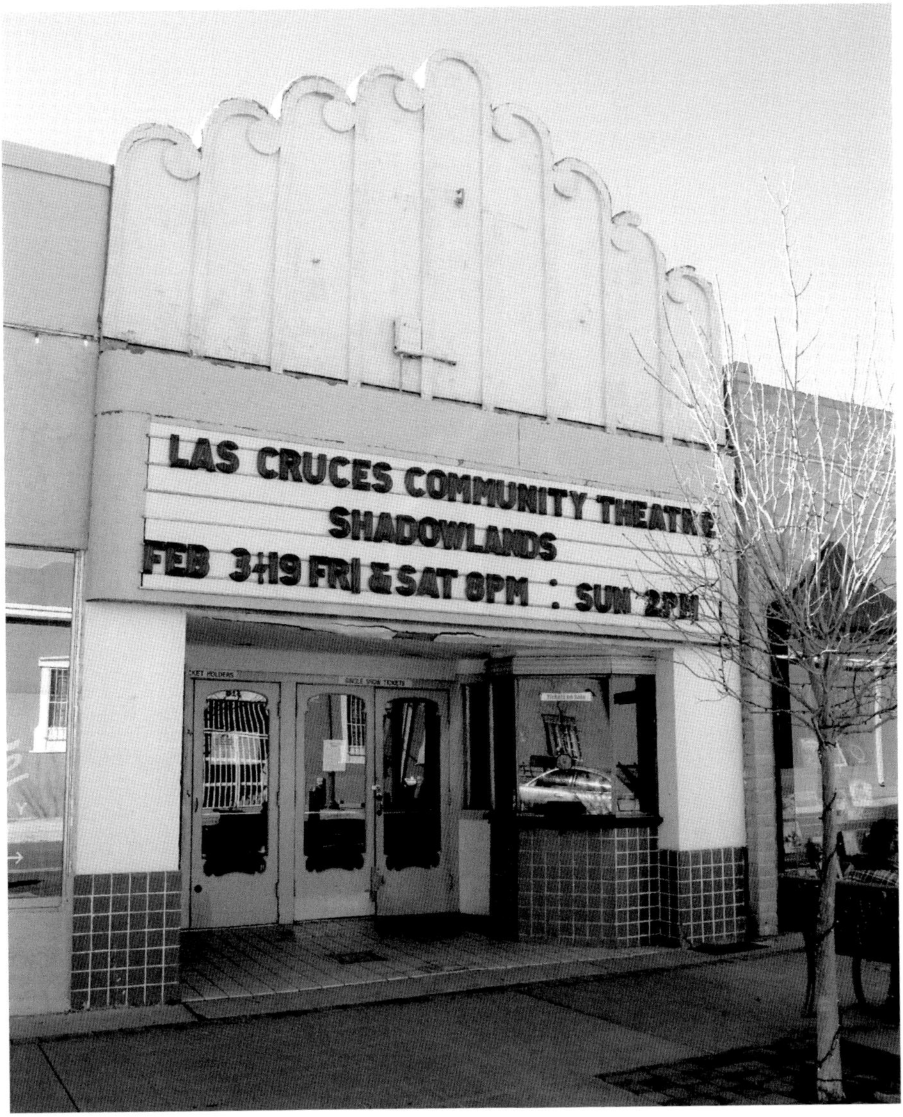

State Theater, now the home of the Las Cruces Community Theatre, Las Cruces. *Randy Carlisle.*

One other theatre that is noted for Las Cruces is the Navajo, which apparently was only open briefly, in 1925, and operated by the Navajo Amusement Company, which also boasted screens in two other New Mexican towns: Socorro (the Gem) and Magdalena (the Casino).

NEW MEXICO'S OLDEST THEATRE

In a little town, just over the other side of the border, at the city limits of Las Cruces, there exists the Fountain Theatre. It has endured for more than one hundred years. The town is Mesilla, and the theatre is rented from a landlord of dubious measure, a very wealthy man who owns the adjacent adobe-style restaurant that serves tourist-style Mexican food to thundering throngs. He is wealthy, and his high-end home was used in the 2016 film *Captain Fantastic*.

The Fountain Theatre has been a cultural hotspot in Mesilla since 1905. At one point during the Civil War, it was a hospital for wounded Confederate soldiers and the headquarters for said army as well (there were several, some large, Civil War battles in New Mexico).

Later, in 1905, it was purchased by Albert Fountain Jr. (the son of Colonel Albert Jennings Fountain), a politician who was murdered in 1897. Fountain Jr.'s body and that of his eight-year-old son were never found. The Fountain family has been associated with Mesilla since 1873, when the colonel moved to Mesilla with his wife, Mariana, and their five children.

The theatre is made of adobe, and there are two hand-painted murals on the long walls parallel to the seating area. It is said that in about 1915, Albert Jr. began painting the murals, which perhaps depict his family arriving in the Mesilla Valley. Completed in 1924, they have been touched up several times since and partially restored as small pieces of the adobe walls crumbled. Later tests noted that the murals were done much later, but sometimes the myth overrides the truth.

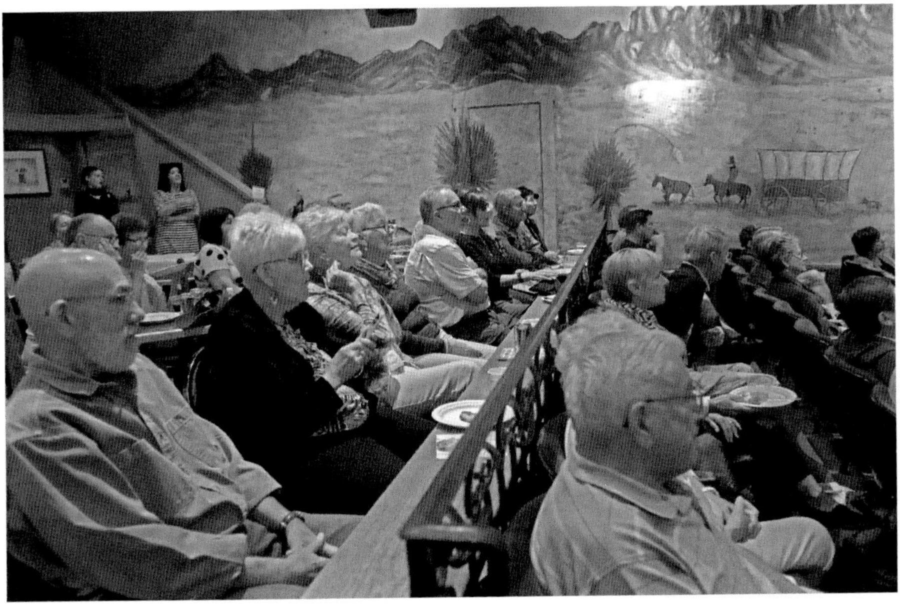

Fountain Theatre patrons, Mesilla. *Robert Yee.*

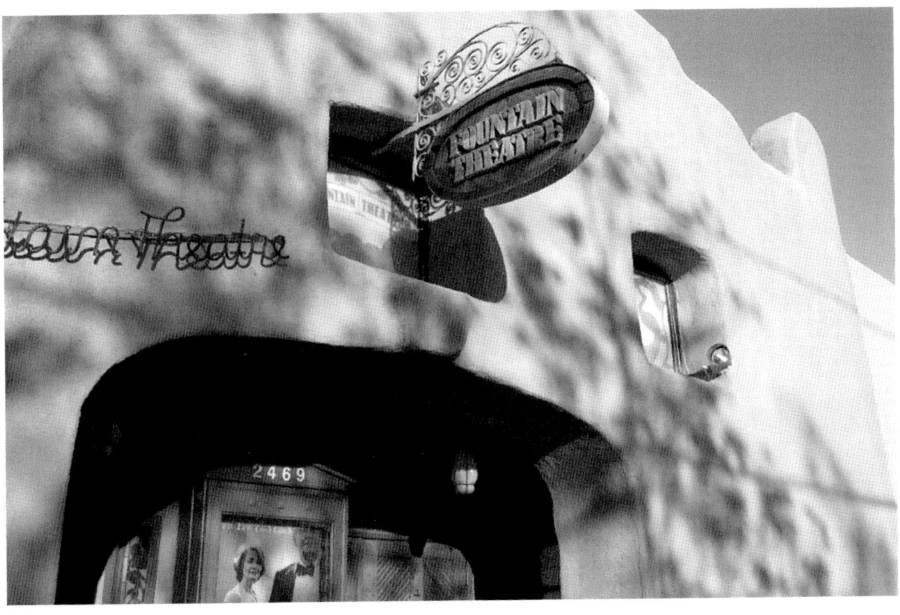

Fountain Theatre exterior. *Robert Yee.*

Previously, in about 1875, the Fountains and Colonel Fountain's brother, Edward Jennings, who was a Shakespearean actor, rented a building a short distance away and opened the new Mesilla Valley Opera House. For some time, this palace thrived on stage plays featuring family theatricals and local talent. The colonel had founded the Mesilla Dramatic Association, renting a building on the northwest corner of the plaza and renovating it with Albert Jr., who also created stage designs and painted sets with his father.

After purchasing the current Fountain Theatre, Albert Fountain Jr. became a producer of plays, opera, vaudeville productions and, as mentioned earlier, lantern slide shows. In 1912, the name was changed to the Fountain of Pleasure, along with modifications that would allow movies to be shown.

It was a family affair, as Albert Jr., his wife and their children created music for the silent films that were screened. With the films having intertitles in English (intertitles are the short slides you read during silent films), Fountain translated the cards to Spanish, as most of the community members were Hispanic or native New Mexican.

The theatre sported a small balcony area that is now the projection booth, and it is said that Albert Jr. was a bit of a card, often adding "his own comments, opinions, or jokes" to presentations.

The venue was operated in this fashion until 1929, when Fountain sold the establishment to a Vicente Guerra, who was the first to show movies with sound at the Fountain. He also installed a projector with the sound equipment, along with a real screen and permanent seats.

Things didn't go well for Guerra, however, and in 1938, he had to give up the building due to foreclosure. Ironically, the bank that took the building sold it to the highest bidder, who happened to be Albert Fountain III. From that point on, until 2008, the theatre remained in the Fountain family until it was sold by an out-of-town member of the family to a local high-rolling realtor. With the realtor knowing nothing of the theatre business and not having a good relationship with the building's leasers, the Mesilla Valley Film Society, which had rented the crumbling building since February 1989 (the Fountain remains the only independent movie theatre for 250 miles in any direction), rallied with community support and was able to remain in the Fountain.

Fountain III's operation of the theatre lasted until 1951, as he showed mostly Spanish-language pictures and the occasional live play. From 1951 to 1963, the theatre was vacant, though occasionally used for storage, including hay.

In the early 1960s, Arthur Fountain acquired the theatre and loaned it to the Las Cruces Community Theatre, which reopened it in 1964, using the building until 1977, when it moved to a different space. From 1977 until the film society moved in, Artie Fountain ran the theatre and occasionally hosted plays as well.

It wasn't until 2014 that the theatre underwent some major repair and renovation that allowed for a better atmosphere for the very successful film society, which is run entirely by volunteers.

A BIT FARTHER SOUTH, in Anthony, the town that straddles two states, a drive-in theatre apparently had a reasonably successful run. It was called the Joy Drive-In, of which little information is available other than it was run by the Garcia family in the mid-1960s; Otilia Garcia served homemade food at the concession stand. The Joy apparently went belly-up in 1975. A photo of the old marquee from 1977 shows posters of several Spanish-language films.

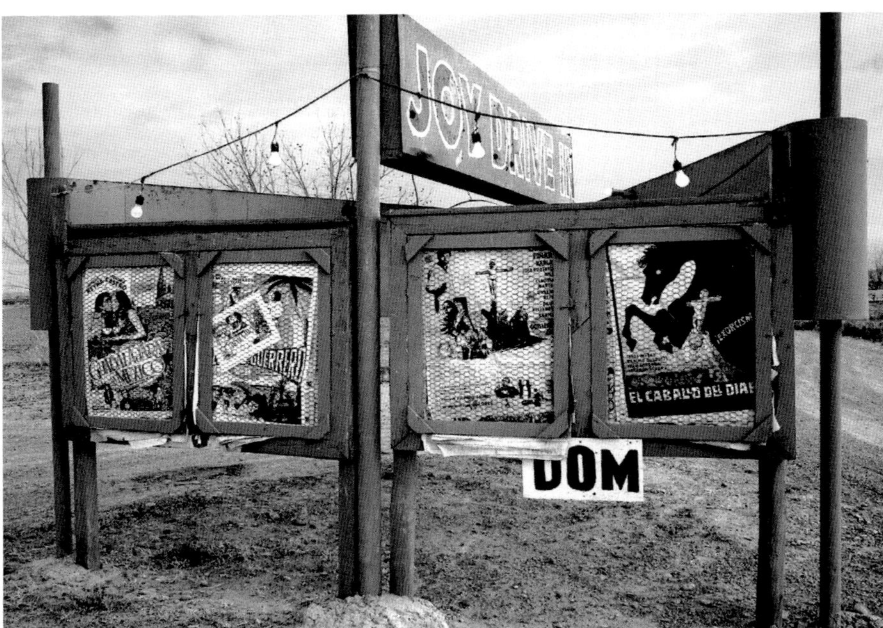

Joy Drive-In. *Bob Christensen.*

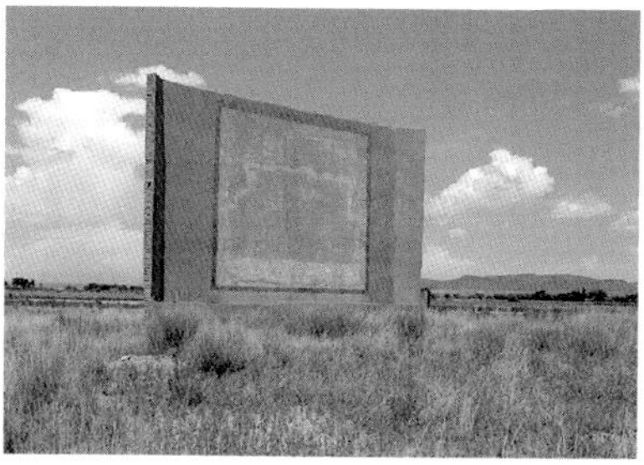

Hatch Drive-In, Hatch. *Bob Christensen.*

The Gem Theater in Anthony might have been in business in about 1926, but no other information is available other than a classified ad in the old *El Paso (TX) Herald.*

North of Las Cruces lies the chile capital of New Mexico, Hatch. While the city is better known for the amazing fruit (some say it is a vegetable, and it's found in almost every recipe that comes from the state), I found a small footnote that mentioned the Hatch Drive-In, with no real opening or closing dates, as well as three indoor theatres: the Bohannon, Mission and Palace. The Bohannon was operated by the Bohannon brothers, and the timeline on the Mission and Palace would make one think that it was the same theatre but with a new name. These venues are long gone, with the Mission apparently being the last, shuttering in 1955.

DEMING, SILVER CITY, LORDSBURG AND SMALLER TOWNS

To the west of Las Cruces, which is the second-largest community in terms of population in New Mexico, there are several smaller towns and villages. The largest of these is Deming, a quiet municipality on Interstate 10. In the early years of cinema, Deming was hopping with moving picture shows that showed mostly silent films.

Before 1930, Deming hosted many movie emporiums, including the Aerodrome, Broadway, Teal, Pastime, Isis, Cody (which burned down in 1918), Comet, Majestic and Rialto. All are long gone, most lasting only a few years.

Now home to a multiplex, Deming's only other theatres between 1930 or 2009 were the El Rancho, later renamed the Sunn (which had a guest appearance in *Gas, Food, Lodging*, a wonderful 1991 movie made in New Mexico), and the Luna, which operated from 1936 to 1964 or '69 (information varies).

The El Rancho/Sunn opened in 1942, seated six hundred and might have closed in 1975, but the records aren't exactly clear. Whatever the case may be, Claudette Colbert was the first to appear on its silver screen, starring in *Skylark* in February 1942.

Deming was also home to the Mimbres Drive-In, which could accommodate two hundred cars and operated from the mid-1950s to the mid-1980s. It is now a trailer park.

Lordsburg, a community with about 2,500 souls, is farther west on I-10, right near the Arizona border. At this writing, the town does not have a

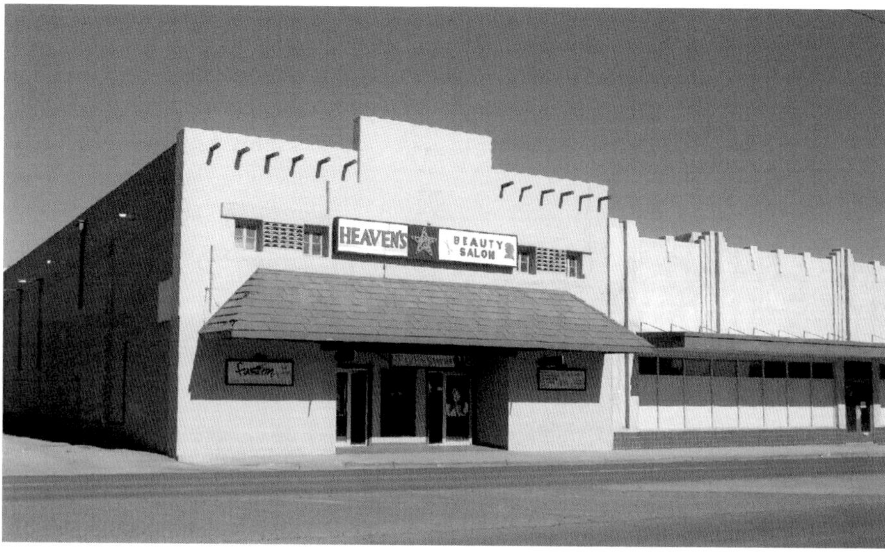

El Rancho/Sunn Cinema, Deming. *Randy Carlisle.*

theatre, but in the past, it hosted several palaces of celluloid, including the funky-looking Coronado, which was, near the end of its lives (the original burned in '88), a twin-screen affair that opened in the late 1940s. After the fire, it settled into a nearby tin building, but it is now closed.

The Palace Theatre is now an auto parts store—a sad statement on the times, I would say. It is said to have had 350 seats and was perhaps open from about 1940 through 1955.

Little is found about the Mesa Theater except that it is long gone, perhaps operating from the mid-1930s until the end of World War II.

The Big Chief Drive-In boasted a single screen and was open from about 1950 to just before 1980. What remains now is the foundation from the projection booth/snack bar and the mounds built for the cars to park on.

There also might have been another film castle, the Studio, which may have been in business in the 1930s, but any evidence is lost to time.

Here's a quick trivia question for you: Can you name the famous film in which the passengers of a certain vehicle were heading for Lordsburg? (The answer is at the end of this section.)

Silver City, the next-largest community in southwestern New Mexico, is a small but thriving town home to Western New Mexico University, many artists and an equal number of cowboy types. Over the course of time, Silver City has seen its share of movie theatres come and go, including Real West

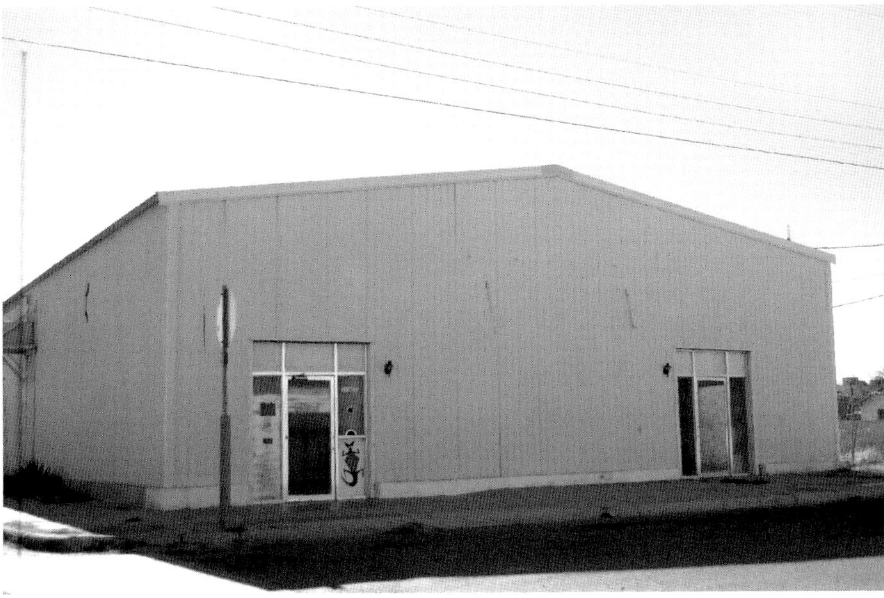

Coronado Theatre, Lordsburg. RIP. *Randy Carlisle.*

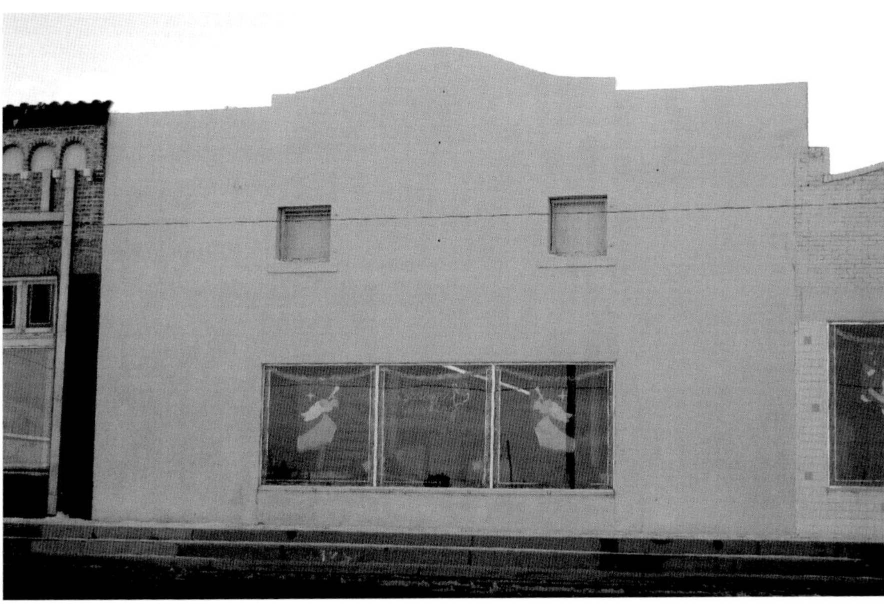

Once upon a time, this was the Palace Theatre in Lordsburg. *Randy Carlisle.*

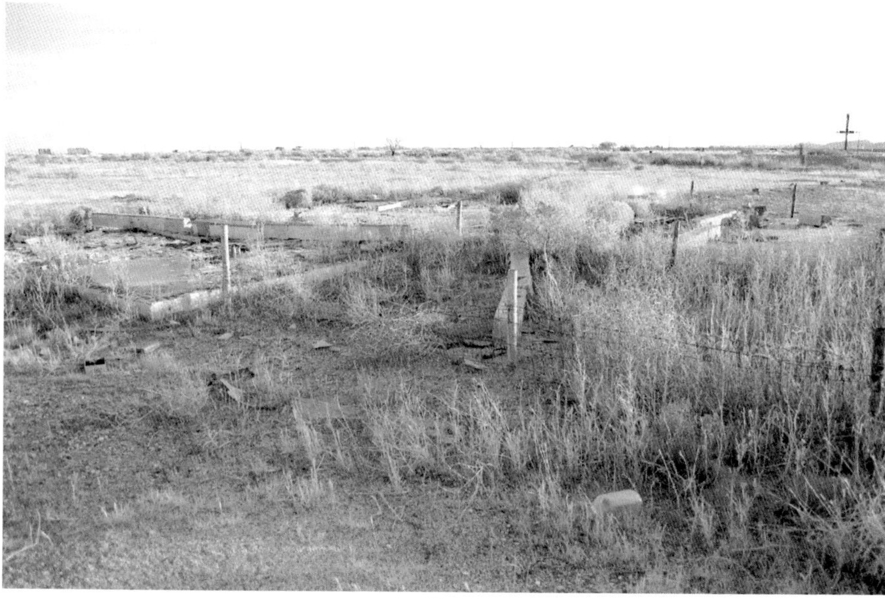

All that remains of Lordsburg's Big Chief Drive-In. *Randy Carlisle.*

Cinema II (2001–13), El Sol (1934–2002), the Gila (1950–2003) and the Silver Sky Vue, Copper and Sundowner Drive-Ins (1950–80 and 1969–85, respectively, for the latter two). Another movie theatre, the Airdome, offered silent films in about 1909 and was "relieved" in 1912 by the Princess, where movies were shown until the building was demolished in 1923.

The Sky Vue once even hosted an Easter service in 1970. Maybe it was praying for more business, which never came. The ideally named Sundowner has also been torn down and most recently was the home of an RV dealership.

The El Sol was in the heart of downtown Silver City and offered about three hundred seats. It was built in ninety days using recycled bricks and was designed, built and owned by local businesspeople. It had an interesting life—including having murals painted on the interior walls by a local art student in the 1940s, when a renovation took place. In the 1950s, the El Sol opened and closed several times, perhaps suffering from competition from the nearby Gila Theatre. Apparently, the auditorium was closed for many years and used as warehouse and storage space for several businesses. Purchased in 1998 by the Medina family, who also owned the Gila at the time, it again received a major face-lift but was closed again in 2002, not long after the Gila also went under.

The El Sol sat silent for many years, but in 2015, it was purchased by Teresa Dahl-Bradine and is now home to a local theatre troupe, the Virus Theater. In need of some renovation, the group is an active fundraiser and rents out the space to other non-movie groups.

The Gila, a cavernous place with more than five hundred seats, had many owners over the years from its opening in 1950 by the locally operated Silco chain. That chain also owned the old Silco Theater, which opened in 1926 in Silver City and is now open again after closing as a movie house in the 1960s and becoming a furniture store. It failed in the 1990s and was sold to the Medinas in 1995, closing again in 2003.

As noted on the website Off the Road in New Mexico (offtheroadnm.org), "in 2013, the Town of Silver City and Silver City Main Street purchased the property with the assistance of a state capital outlay grant from the New Mexico Main Street program." The Silco was built on the lot where the Airdome and Princess once entertained.

The small satellite communities around Silver City (mostly mining towns) also welcomed movies for many years. Arenas Valley, a tad east of Silver City, was home to the Copper Drive-In, of which there is little information other than that it was operating in the mid-1960s. The Bayard, located in the village of Bayard, delighted up to 250 patrons, but only for a short time

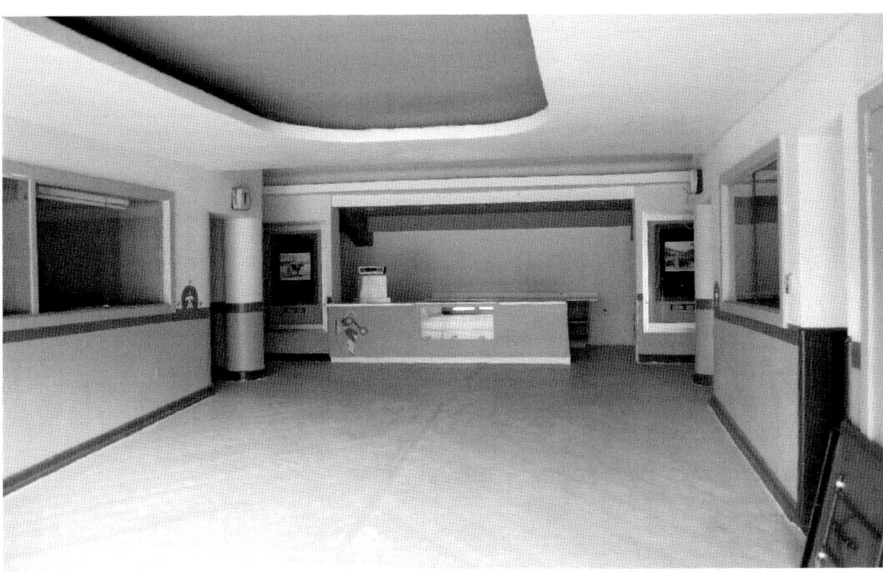

Gila Theatre interior, Silver City. *Randy Carlisle.*

in the early 1950s. A village now known as Santa Clara (but once tagged Central or Central City) may have had a 125-seater that operated in the late 1940s, closing in 1950. It had the very original name of the Central. Nearby Hurley saw the Tejo (formerly the Hurley) operate from about 1915 through 1961. Once owned by Gibraltar Enterprises, it could seat 325 derrieres of all sizes. As of 2014, the foundations remained after the building was removed in 1958, being hauled to and partially recycled in Deming, New Mexico.

There is also a brief mention in the June 17, 1916 edition of *Moving Picture World* that a certain J.P. Gooding, operator of the Hurley Theater, "had plans drawn up for a new $10,000 theater." Several paragraphs down in the same issue, on a much lesser and repulsive note, it was announced that "Miss E Johnson, owner of the Key Theater at Houston, Tex., is building a new theatre at the corner of Milam and Travis streets, in Houston to be called the Lincoln and it is to be for colored people only. This is the most expensive house for colored people on record in the South." It operated until 1977 before being demolished and turned into a parking lot.

A posting on the website Cinema Treasures (cinematreasures.org) by "thisisjohnbook" offered this interesting tidbit about the El Cobre (copper in Spanish) Theater, which was in Santa Rita, New Mexico, now a ghost town: "The theater was like many of the times and included an usher. In this case, this theater, which held 317 people, was segregated, with the 'brown' people sitting on the left. The area was known for its copper, which brought people to town to work at the mine. One source says the theater was demolished in 1961 and essentially Santa Rita became a ghost town. That area is now known as the Chino mine so there are few remnants of a theater or town."

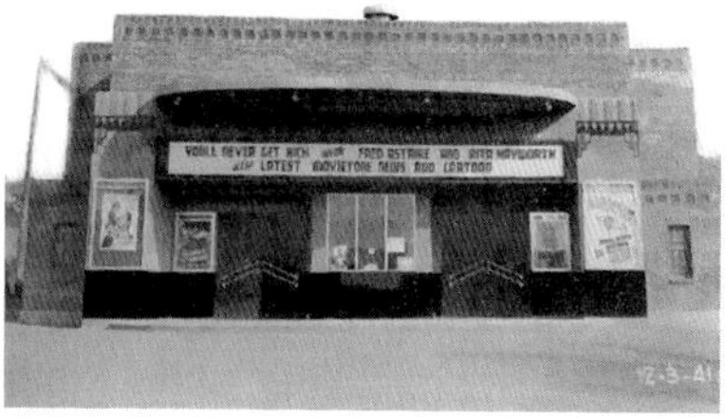

El Cobre, Santa Rita. *From Cinema Treasures, contributed by Ken Roe.*

Perhaps only a rumor, but the tiny community of Hillsboro may have had two claims to fame: being a stop on one of the last stagecoach lines in the United States, which ran as late as 1918, and possibly the home of the Hill Drive-In. There is no real information on this place, other than that it might have been open in 1955.

North and west of Silver City, there exists a lot of beautiful land, including the Gila Wilderness. The ghost town of

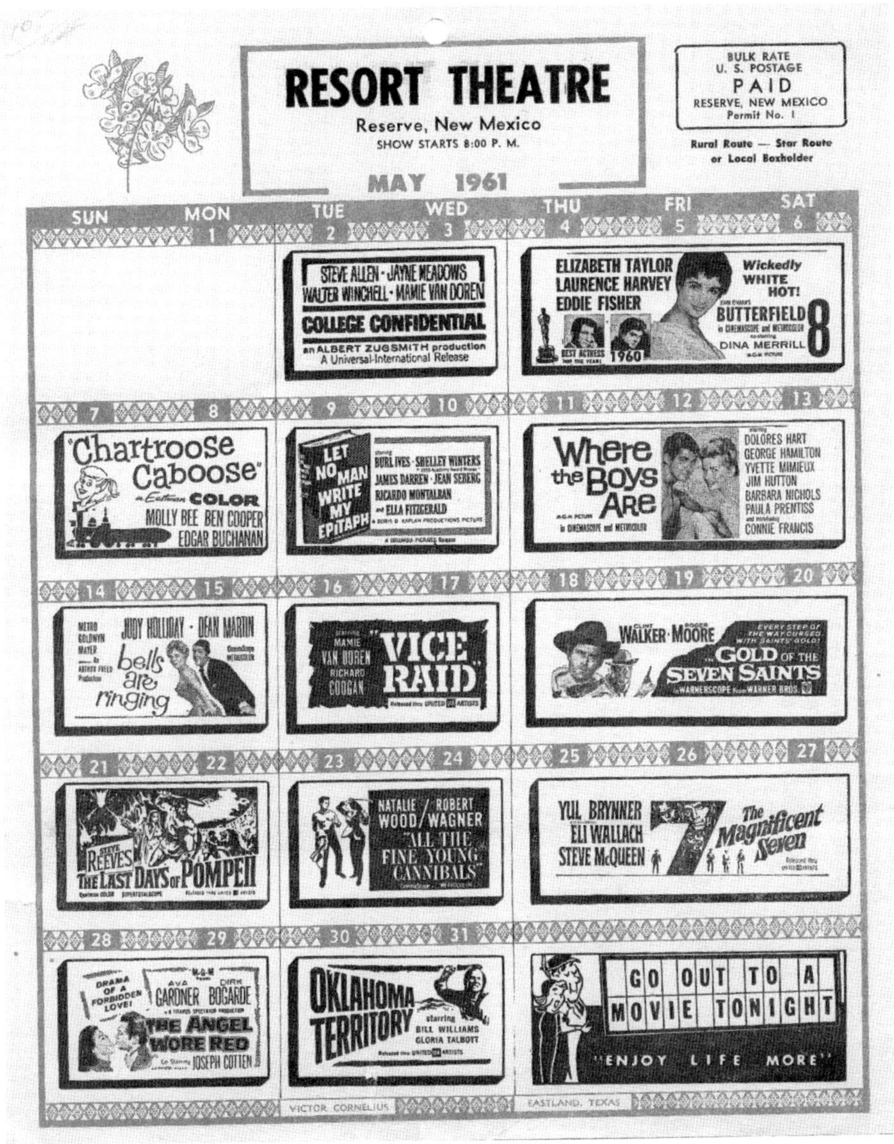

Monthly schedule for Resort Theatre, Reserve. *Author's collection.*

Fierro (iron in Spanish) once had a silent movie theatre run by John Oglesby, who also was a miner, as reported in volume 42 of *Mining and Engineering World* (1915), which noted that "John and Walter Oglesby have opened up a 1-ft streak of fine ore on the Balback mine at a depth of 90 feet."

The small town of Reserve did have the Resort Theatre, which apparently operated in the late 1950s and at least as late as 1961, seating 385, which is almost the entire population of the town.

How about another trivia question: what movie theatre in New Mexico is the hardest to get to, and when was it opened? The answer (cheating a bit here) is the Mogollon Theater, formerly the Midway, located in the ghost town of Mogollon, New Mexico. It opened in 1915 or so and for many years laid claim to be "the oldest intact movie house in New Mexico," even though it wasn't showing films. In 2013, the town was hit by a terrible flood, and renovations have been underway ever since. Mogollon was also where Henry Fonda alighted to shoot portions of the Euro-western *My Name Is Nobody* in 1973. The film co-stars Terrence Hill and was a comedy, with a bit of drama tossed in, about a washed-up gunfighter.

The answer to the earlier trivia question is, of course, *Stagecoach* with John Wayne! It along with two other famous westerns used New Mexico as a place or destination but were not filmed here. The other two films are *High Noon* and *Albuquerque*.

CENTRAL NEW MEXICO

For moviegoers, the next hot spot for theatres is the community of Truth or Consequences, located east and a tad north of Silver City on Interstate 25. The town, formerly known as Hot Springs, achieved its fifteen minutes of fame from a radio show (later a television show) when Ralph Edwards, the producer of *Truth or Consequences*, challenged any community in the United States to change its name to Truth or Consequences. Hot Springs wasn't much of a hot spot, one might say, although it has a lovely location and several soothing hot springs in which to dip. But business was slow.

The website Legends of America (legendsofamerica.com) noted, "The idea started when Ralph Edwards pulled his staff together and said, 'I wish that some town in the United States liked and respected our show so much that it would like to change its name to "Truth or Consequences."' When the New Mexico State Tourist Bureau got wind of the idea, they relayed the news to the Hot Springs Chamber of Commerce and the news spread like wildfire. The chamber and the locals liked the idea of free advertising."

The city soon held an election, the town's name was changed and in no time Edwards and his entire NBC production crew arrived in the newly named city, airing the first live coast-to-coast broadcast of *Truth or Consequences* from the "new" city of Truth or Consequences. One city official in 1950 quipped, "It is the truth that we have the health-giving waters here. The consequences are that people get results."

T or C, as it is commonly called nowadays, also has a movie theatre history, including the El Rio, which probably was open from the 1950s until

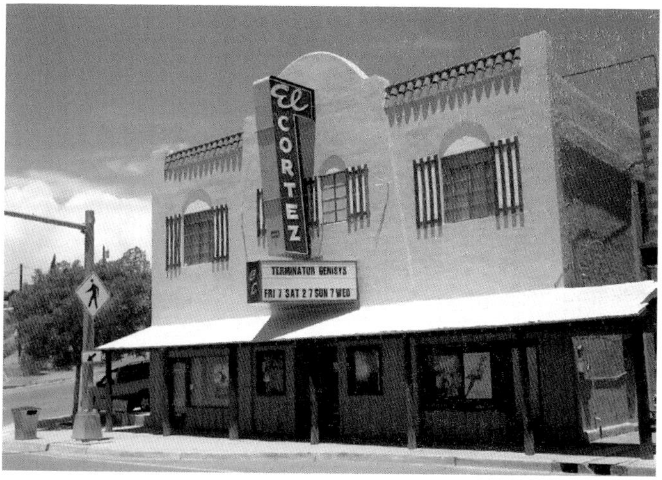

El Cortez, Truth or Consequences. *From iamnm.com.*

about 2000. It was a three-story affair, and the owners, back during the VHS days, were smart and opportunistic, renting VCRs to the public while renting them videos as well.

The El Cortez was built in 1941 and, not much later, suffered a gas explosion that blew off the front part of the theatre. However, it was repaired and reopened. For many years, until about 1995, it was in and out of business. It was slightly expanded in the early years, going from 500 to 580 seats. In 2007, the theatre found new owners, who have kept the masses entertained since then, mostly on weekends, with a smaller renovated auditorium that holds about 125 popcorn lovers.

Two drive-ins might have also been in business in T or C, but information is scant about the Palms (possibly open from 1955 to 1975) and the Jet, which might have had a brief lifespan in the mid-1960s. Still another mystery theatre is the Rialto, which may have operated briefly from the mid-1930s until the end of World War II.

HERE'S ANOTHER TRIVIA QUESTION: where was the 1997 film *Truth or Consequences, N.M.*, which made a whopping $55,000 at the box office, filmed? A) Truth or Consequences, New Mexico, or B) Utah and Nevada? (The answer is B.)

FARTHER NORTH

Let's continue on our journey to New Mexico movie theatres farther north, up Interstate 25, to the town of Socorro, home of New Mexico Tech. Oddly, Socorro was theatre-free for an entire decade but was once home to several film palaces. In late 2017, the New Loma reopened, much to the pleasure of local residents. Until then, movie fans had to travel north to the town of Los Lunas—and one must *really* want to see a movie since it is about fifty miles, one way.

Back in the day, however, Socorro had at least one big screen, and in this town, there were several. The "big shue," the Loma, opened in the 1920s. Although it had been ready to open a few years earlier, in 1918, the state health department quarantined it due to the Spanish flu outbreak. That was lifted in 1919, suggesting that the theatre might have opened then rather than the 1920s, when it was certainly in business.

The original name of the cinema was the Guild Theater. It was owned by George Keith and managed by M.E. Pickens, who renamed the hall the Gem Theater, as Socorro was then known as the "Gem City." It was renovated, received upgraded equipment in 1932 and flourished, even during the Great Depression. In 1937, it was sold to a chain, Gibraltar Entertainment, which promptly closed it for several months for more upgrades and a new name, Loma. During the grand opening of the screen, the local daily, the *Chieftain*, proudly announced that it now had both men's and women's restrooms. How's that for progress?

Tragically, the Loma and several adjoining buildings were destroyed by fire just before Christmas 1956. A posting on the Cinema Treasures site offers the news story of that day from the *Chieftain*:

> *TWO HUNDRED ESCAPE THEATRE FIRE AT SOCORRO*
> *Fire broke up a showing of "The Day the World Ended"* [how ironic] *and 200 theater patrons escaped safely as the flames destroyed three businesses here last night. The blaze raged for three hours before being brought under control about 10 p.m. Firemen from Magdalena and the New Mexico Institute of Mining and Technology joined the Socorro volunteer department in fighting the fire that may have caused loss as high as $200,000.*
>
> *Destroyed were the Loma Theater, the B&B Pool Hall and the Midway Garage, where the fire is thought to have originated. Firemen were able to save one of New Mexico's historic buildings, the Park Hotel, which is on the same block with the theater, garage and pool hall.*
>
> *People in the theater said they had smelled smoke about 20 minutes before they were told to evacuate the building. A sudden puff of smoke filled the theater as patrons were leaving. There was no panic in the crowd and all persons moved out of the building in an orderly manner. Bill Strong, a Loma Theater employee, estimated damage to the theater alone at $50,000.*

It took until 1958 for the New Loma to open its doors; it was actually a converted armory, operated by Dollison Theaters. The building was owned by the state, and in 1972, it was sold to Socorro's First State Bank to ensure that the movie house would continue to operate. Boasting six hundred seats, the operation was well managed and did a good business until the 1980s, when things began to change dramatically. Cable television and video rentals became quite the thing, and the Loma was reduced in size. The theater had new ownership from 1988 to 1992, and in '92 it was acquired by Trans-Lux, which was one of the bigger chains of the era. Even though the bank still owned the building and cut the fee, even offering free rent, Trans-Lux opted to close the cinema instead, doing so in October 2008.

Socorro was home to the Sierra Drive-In, which was open from 1956 until 1986. It fit two hundred cars and was later called the Sierra Vista. As late as 2014, the screen still stood on the far south end of town, as did the hull of the ticket booth and concession/projection building.

Magdalena is another small community, immediately west of Socorro. It, too, had movie theatres in its history. The Aragon, before burning, may have shown films from 1945 to 1955, seating two hundred happy patrons. The Casino Theater appears to have been open as early as 1921, possibly closing in the 1930s. No other information is available about this movie house.

ROAD TRIP TO EASTERN NEW MEXICO

We'll cut across US 60 and head for the eastern part of the state now. The small municipality of Carrizozo is the first stop, once home to the Nike Drive-In, which is on the west side of town. According to a contribution by Bob Meza on the website Cinema Tour, "The Nike [was] located on Hwy 380. The snack bar has been converted to a house with the projection booth portholes still intact and used as windows. The capacity was 200 [cars] and it was owned by William Skelton." Sounds like a house I could live in.

The Central Theater also receives a brief note, although it may not have even existed, as research reveals nothing about this silver screen palace.

On a better note, the Lyric, which was also known as the Carrizozo and Crystal over the years, operated for many years and might once again open. When known as the Carrizozo, it was mostly an opera and vaudeville place, and it wasn't until 1918 that a new owner purchased the facility and started showing the movie *Till I Come Back to You* on Christmas night of that year.

Just a few blocks away, another entrepreneur, George J. Dingwall, began screening moving pictures in the back room of the Exchange Bank, while the Carrizozo concentrated on live performances. That building still exists and is the Masonic Temple, as well as home to the Lincoln County (NM) Historical Society. Dingwall later purchased the Carrizozo and began showing films in that venue.

In the summer of 1931, the theatre became the Lyric and screened its first sound movie, *The Last Parade* with Boris Karloff. The theatre name went back and forth from Lyric to Crystal over the years, but in the end, 1979, neither helped and the movies were gone from the town of 1,100. At that time, the operation was run by the Carrizozo Association for the Performing Arts. The building was auctioned to an unknown buyer in 1981. There is a possibly apocryphal story that says the death knell for the cinema came with a local rating dispute over *The Exorcist*. No concrete story is available, but one never knows what will rile up folks.

Paula Wilson purchased the building in 2016 and, with community support, is slowly but surely renovating the old theatre via various fundraisers. No timetable is set for the opening of the house of celluloid, but let's hope that Wilson and partners are successful.

Almost every other community in the area had a theatre at one time or another as well. South of Carrizozo, in Tularosa, the Jet Drive-In, which could welcome two hundred cars, kept people up at night and was operating in 1957, when it played *Seven Men from Now* in late May. It was a single-screen place, with the screen still standing as late as 1983. It may have closed around 1984—but again, not much history is available.

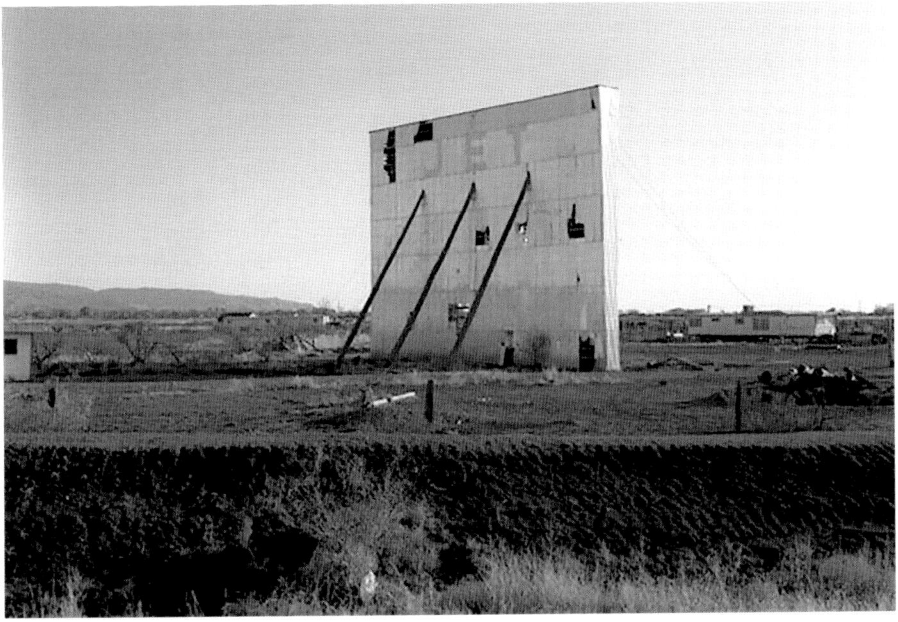

Jet Drive-In, Tularosa. *Steven Fitch.*

The interestingly named Muse-U also might have allowed for necking in the balcony, if it indeed had one, since very little is now known about this cinema. It possibly was open starting in 1930 and was still showing cinematic delights in the spring of 1957. It is said to have had 250 seats and might have had the same owner as the Jet.

Other cities, villages and towns in south-central New Mexico had theatres. Capitan is said to have been the home of the Coronado in the mid-1940s. The Lodge and/or Pavilion Theaters were located in Cloudcroft, a tiny mountain resort town. And in one of the bigger towns of the area, Ruidoso, there may have been as many as three indoor theatres and two drive-ins.

The indoor cinemas included the Camelot (said to have been the entrance to a failed planned community), which housed a two-screen theatre in the façade. It operated in the 1980s, as I found an e-mail to a guy who posted a picture of the Dupont Castle, noting that the current resident (in 2010) lived there and used some of the building to rent out as mini-storage. A response to that posting asking for more information came a few years later from a guy who said he had seen *Labyrinth* (1986) and *Snow White* (1987) there; after the place closed, he and some friends would sneak in through a hole in the roof. "I recall there being lots of film negatives lying around," he offered.

Also in Ruidoso was the Mountain View Drive-In, which may have operated from the mid-1950s to about 1980 before becoming a drive-up church, the Pueblo, with four hundred seats; it screened such gems as *Huk!* and *Baby Doll* but also had some great films such as *Friendly Persuasion* and *The Bad Seed* in May 1957. The monthly calendar encouraged viewers to head to the "Chocolate Shop" located next door after the show, which must have been open mighty late!

The Mount Vine Drive-In, long defunct, was in a "suburb" of Ruidoso, Ruidoso Downs, home of the famed horse racing track. No immediate information is available, other than that it was probably owned by a gentleman named Joe Yates, was small and was open in 1969, if not before or after.

Heading a bit farther south again, we find the city of Alamogordo, which has been very active in the comings and goings of movie palaces. While researching, I often found myself wondering the motivation behind someone wanting to open a movie theatre. Of course, the usual idea is to make money, but many small independent theatres that are still in operation are now nonprofits and the trend to "micro-cinemas" is on the rise. Micro-cinemas usually have fifty or so seats and a unique selection of concessions, often offering wine and beer. At this writing, New Mexico hasn't latched on to this concept, but there is a lot of potential in several cities and towns around the country.

But Alamogordo has also seen its share of theatres come and go, such as the Sierra, which opened in the spring of 1956 with a screening of *The Lieutenant Wore Skirts*. It lasted until perhaps the 1980s, when it was purchased by a local resident, Margaret Flickinger, who in turn donated the auditorium to a local arts group. The venue stopped showing movies and remains a multipurpose venue, offering plays and concerts; it now seats nearly six hundred guests. It was once the home of the White Sands Film Festival, which later moved to Las Cruces.

The Sands Theatre, also known as the White Sands Theatre due to Alamogordo's proximity to the amazing and beautiful White Sands National Monument, had 422 seats. It went through several different owners over the years, all of whom were corporate and closed in 1985. The Historic Sands Theatre website (historicsandstheatre.com) offers this bit of history about the place: "The White Sands Theater opened in the 1920s as an open-air theater. It was used mainly as an overflow for the Alamento Theatre on nearby 10th street. During hot summer evenings, it was widely used, as the Alamento was far too hot to enjoy a movie. In the 1930s a roof was added. It boosted of having a water-cooled loft that kept the entire theater air-conditioned. The original capacity was 210 seats. The Sands closed its doors in the early 1980s."

Nearly thirty years later, in 2013, the hall opened again as an occasional movie theatre, mostly offering second runs of major titles and is also a live performance space. It is owned by Vision Broadcasting. Here's two other tidbits of information about this interesting place: it uses a vintage Manley popcorn machine from the 1950s, and in 1981, a drunk driver careened into the theatre, unfortunately killing one person. From UPI.com: "A teenager watching a horror film from the back row of a movie theater was killed by a car that careened through the lobby and smashed through a rear wall....Donna Howard Thon, 40, of Alamogordo, was charged with vehicular homicide and driving while intoxicated....James Malone, 17, was crushed beneath the car, which careened into the lobby and smashed through the rear wall of the darkened Sands Theater late Thursday. Alamogordo Police Lt. Ray Bailey said Malone was found five rows forward from the impact area."

No other tragedies were reported at other Alamogordo theatres of yesteryear, including the Mesa, which was owned and operated by Theater

Enterprises, which made history in 1953 when it was involved in a lawsuit that went to the U.S. Supreme Court, challenging the practice of the times for studios to only screen new releases on big city screens, thus creating a monopoly for the bigger chains and studios that, at the time, often owned theatres too. Although Theater Enterprises lost, this did open a door to needed change in the distribution of films, which remains an issue to this day.

The Alamento Theatre, again with a little historical uniqueness, opened in 1917, showed *Why Change Your Wife* in July 1921 and was still around in June 1950 when it screened the great film noir *Side Street.* It apparently became the Mesa just a few weeks later, replete with a front recycled from a theatre in Lovington, New Mexico, owned by the same company that was now running the Mesa. Upon its opening, it could fit 350 folks.

Several drive-ins popped up around town as well, with the Yucca surviving for about sixteen years, from 1954 to 1970, although some sources say it was open until 1985. It was a large space, welcoming about 450 cars to view its sixty-two- by forty-four-foot screen. The Yucca was owned by Mr. and Mrs. Marshall Sanguinet, who also operated the Starlite Drive-In on the other side of town. It changed hands in 1955 and became much smaller, allowing only 200 autos. Both places were later operated by Commonwealth Theatres, with the Starlite closing in 1985. At one time, Commonwealth was the sixth-largest theatre chain in the country, with 425 screens.

The Cinema 5 (1987–2007) was usurped by the Aviator 10, which is owned and operated by Allen Theatres, a very local and very large New Mexico–based chain. The Aviator has the distinction of being the first set of screens in New Mexico to go completely digital.

HEADING FARTHER EAST

Our tour continues east, with a brief stop in Cloudcroft, New Mexico, a resort town located in the beautiful Sacramento Mountains. It is a popular place for Texans to vacation or weekend, seeking relief from the heat and flatness of far west Texas. Cloudcroft may have had a theatre, the Pavilion, in about 1900 or so, but no historical record to confirm this can be found. The Lodge, a beautiful resort, was host to some famous names in the movie world, including Clark Gable, Judy Garland and Gilbert Roland. In those years, the Lodge was managed by none other than hotel magnate Conrad Hilton.

The next major town after Alamogordo and the mountains is the never changing town of Artesia, located on the oil-burdened flats of eastern New Mexico. Artesia was the first town where I resided in New Mexico, when I briefly attended the now defunct College of Artesia. And I'm not telling you when that was.

During my first soiree away from home, I learned a lot. Artesia was small and isolated, offering one theatre, and I saw almost everything it played, including a few "spaghetti" westerns (westerns made in Spain mostly by Italian film crews back in the days). I saw many of these pictures at the magnificent Land of the Sun Theater.

Opened in 1947, it apparently was a state-of-the-art theatre for the times, owned by the Gilchrist family until 1975. Not only was it a cool Art Deco–like theatre, but it was also the first theatre I ever attended that served dill pickles and allowed smoking. Sometime after '75, the venue became part of the Carmike chain, eventually needing renovations on all levels.

In 2001, in conjunction with Artesia MainStreet, Carmike agreed to rejuvenate the inside, while MainStreet would handle the façade and the fantastic neon sign. The name had also changed, perhaps to Cinema Twin. (The nine-hundred-seat auditorium was made into a two-screen venue at some point.)

The Land of the Sun had a touch of infamy in August 1966 when it canceled its showings of the Beatles movie *Help!* after a magazine article appeared in which John Lennon suggested that the Beatles were more popular than Jesus. Some months before, the comment had appeared in a teenage fan magazine, *Datebook*. Lennon's comment was ignored by the English press. But upon the group's arrival in the United States some five months later, Christian groups reacted with ire and a "Ban the Beatles" campaign began.

Lennon's comment was as follows: "Christianity will go. It will vanish and shrink. I needn't argue about that; I know I'm right and I will be proved right. We're more popular than Jesus now. I don't know which will go first—rock & roll or Christianity. Jesus was all right, but his disciples were thick and ordinary. It's them twisting it that ruins it for me."

KZEE radio, located in Weatherford, Texas, is said to have "damned their songs eternally." Lennon later apologized and clarified, but the Beatles' shining moment at the Land of the Sun had already seen its sunset. Today, the theatre is run by AMC, still has two screens and is the only movie house in town.

The other big theatre in town was the Ocotillo. However, it had ceased screening flickers long before my arrival in Artesia. It is now the Ocotillo Performing Arts Center, built in the early 1930s and opening in 1935 as the Ocotillo Cinema. It is said that it was a very popular movie house that "became a local gathering spot" until its closure in 1959. In 1961, the building was reopened as Clifton's Cafeteria and then became Townhouse Cafeteria in 1964.

The Artesia Arts Council was incorporated as a 501(c)(3) nonprofit organization in 1975 and began to work with a group of ten founding patrons and fifty-four charter members, planning art shows, workshops and other events. Finally, in 2001, with the support of the community, the Arts Council purchased the Townhouse Cafeteria building. A capital campaign began, and over the next few years, enough funding was raised to renovate the old movie house into the Ocotillo Performing Arts Center.

Artesia was also home to a few drive-in theatres. The Circle, which opened sometime in the early 1950s, had a name change to the Hermosa before shutting down in 1985. It could fit 350 cars and may have had the same ownership as Land of the Sun.

The silent era was in full swing when Artesia became home to the Apollo Theater in the early years. The only readily available information on this movie palace is an ad in the *Pecos Valley News* from December 1915. The Majestic Theatre was also in business in 1913, but it is unclear whether it had live performance only or if it included silent cinema and how long it lasted.

Heading south from Artesia on the straight four-lane highway to Carlsbad, home of the beautiful Carlsbad Caverns National Park, where about twenty films and television shows have been shot (at least in part), I have found that over the years, about ten theatres that have come and gone.

One of the most interesting is the Cavern Theatre, which opened in 1951 but ceased operating sometime in the 1990s. Currently, the City of Carlsbad owns it, thanks to the generosity of the two families who owned the building, the Lights and the Rogerses, who donated it in 2014 with hopes of having it turned into a multipurpose entertainment venue.

It is said that the Cavern was designed in the International style, a form of modernism that featured minimal ornamentation and streamlined forms. The Cavern had a large, multicolored, neon marquee and murals of local landmarks painted on the inside walls. It also had a large balcony, perfect for necking or tossing Jujubes from. All told, it has more than five hundred seats. As of mid-2017, the renovation is underway, with plans for live stage performances and films as well, starting in late 2019.

The Cavern also had the honor of hosting the world premiere of *The Honkers* in mid-1972. It is the only feature film shot entirely in and around the city of Carlsbad and is a pretty decent comedy-drama about a washed-up rodeo star, played by James Coburn, accompanied by his friend and "savior," played by former New Mexico resident Slim Pickens (best remembered for his role in *Dr. Strangelove* where he rode the nuclear bomb that was dropped).

Carlsbad's other cinematic claim to fame is the Fiesta Drive-In, which boasts three screens, the only operating drive-in in New Mexico that has more than a single screen. Originally opening in 1948, it closed in 1970, not reopening until 1990, this time with the three screens and a lot of popularity.

The Cinema Treasures site has the following post about the theatre, which is owned by the Rogers family, probably the same folks who donated the Cavern Theater to the city: "The massive original screen tower had a mural of a Mexican man and woman dancing, and was animated with neon lighting. Above them was the theater's name in Streamline style lettering. By 1955 it was operated by Frontier Theatres....The Fiesta Drive-In closed in 1970, but was completely rebuilt in 1989 as a three-screen drive-in with parking for over 600 cars, FM stereo sound, and a modern concession stand. The Fiesta Drive-In was open Friday through Monday year-round, but had closed by 2010. It was re-opened in the summer of 2012." It seems to be thriving, despite carping by patrons on the theatre's Facebook page. Most of the complaints are silly and pointless, since most people can't tell time or read posted signs.

The single-screen Big Sky Drive-In could handle a whopping eight hundred cars and was in operation from 1960 to 1980; it now has gone from glory to bad times, as the site is now home to a Walmart. (Boo! Hiss!)

Things are big in Carlsbad, such as the Cactus Theatre, which could hold 935 happy people and did so from 1934 until 1969. The building is now demolished and had quite a history of owners, with four different corporations booking the movies and paying the bills.

The short-lived Corral Drive-In, now the site of a Lowe's Home Improvement Store, was owned and operated by Ray and Bill Bartlett. However, their venture didn't last long, opening in 1951 and going out of business in 1955. The Bartletts also owned an indoor theatre of the same name, which might have been the Cavern, possibly opening as early as 1930 and lasting until '51.

A much more successful enterprise was the father-and-son team the Crawfords, who once owned all the theatres in Carlsbad during the 1950s and 1960s. In 1975, they sold their holdings to Frontier Theatres, which later merged with Commonwealth Theaters, a one-time major player in the theatre world.

Located in the long-gone Crawford Hotel, the Crawford Theater was probably Carlsbad's first movie theatre and was operated by A.J. Crawford, opening in 1917. It changed hands several times and in 1931 was still in business, offering five hundred seats to happy moviegoers. It is not clear when the theatre closed, but it certainly has.

The Eddy Theater was another large movie palace, hosting up to 800 guests. Information about its dates of operation are scarce, as are those for the Tower, which opened in 1939 and closed in the late 1950s. The *Film Daily Yearbook* of 1951 lists the Tower Theatre as being operated by Theatre Enterprises Inc. and seating 750, but later it was operated by Ray Bartlett. A Wells Fargo parking lot occupies most of the Tower property today.

Even less information is available about the Yucca Twin Drive-In, which was operated by Commonwealth in the early and mid-1980s. So, don't try to go there.

FAR EAST

Jal, Tatum, Eunice and Lovington are all small communities that dot the flat, oil derrick–bedecked plains of far southeastern New Mexico. Each town had a theatre or two at one time or another.

Jal, named after rancher John A. Lynch, is a town of about two thousand. It was home to the now demolished Rex Theater, located on Main Street, and had 375 seats. Built in 1938 by Griffith Theatres, which at one time or another controlled nearly thirty screens, it was sold to C.C. Caldwell of Texas, who owned it from 1945 to 1955 before selling it to Bruce Wilkerson and Morris Woods. The Rex was managed by Mary Lou and Hal Betty until 1957, when it was sold once again, this time to Theatre Enterprises, another big operation from the 1940s and 1950s. On July 8, 1962, it burned to the ground, the fire being so intense that the volunteer firefighters across the street barely had time to react to the blaze. It should be noted that the fire started after the last show of the day and no one was injured, fortunately.

Two drive-ins should be noted: the Panther, probably named after the local high school team, and the Jal. Both were said to be single-screen operations, and both were demolished. A few minor bits of information about the operations exist: 225 cars could fit at the Panther, which was also owned by Theatre Enterprises, was owned by the operators of the Rex prior to that and was later owned by Frontier Theatres; the Jal might have been in business in the mid-1980s. No other information has been found about that screen.

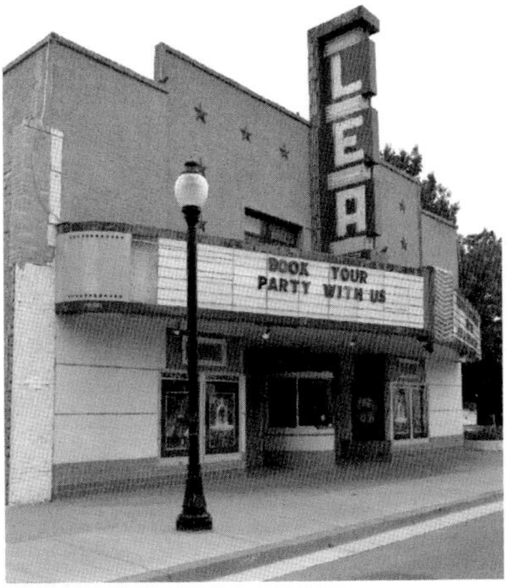

This page: Lea Theater, Lovington. *Lea County Museum, Jim Harris.*

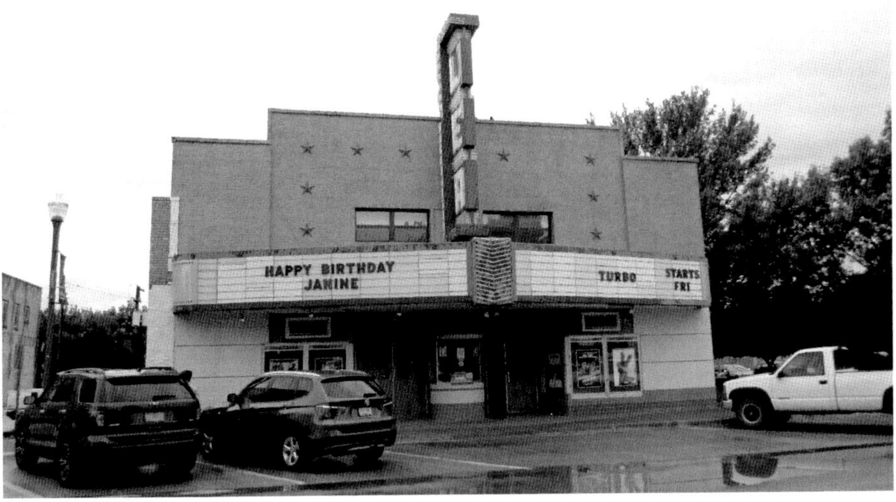

Eunice, New Mexico, a short distance north of Jal, is another small oil town and became home to the Star Drive-In, closed and demolished, and the Lea, which was apparently in business from about 1940 to 1955 and was also part of the two big groups of theatres in New Mexico, Griffith and Theater Enterprises. Size-wise, it could hold almost 450 patrons, a quarter of the population of Eunice.

Lovington, another cattle and oil town that has done a lot of work to preserve its small-town atmosphere, has done well to keep its Lea Theater operating over the years—but not all of them. The website Cinema Tour noted that "the Lea Theater opened in 1948 as 'one of the finest, small-city movie houses in the United States,' its boosters proclaimed. In stark contrast to the surrounding buildings that line the courthouse square, the Lea's modern touches made it a stand-out."

The Lea was built by R.E. Griffith Theaters Inc., a regional theatre chain based in Dallas. Business boomed at the Lea throughout the 1950s. The town's population nearly doubled after the discovery of oil nearby at the South Lovington Pool. The Lea, like many of New Mexico's theatres, hosted numerous civic events and, during the 1950s, even a Miss and Mrs. America contest, where women were judged on appearance, homemaking abilities and poise (which is also how I picked my wife).

The theatre changed hands in the 1960s and went dark in the late 1980s. Reopened after an extensive restoration in 1991 by the Joy family, it won the New Mexico MainStreet "Best Building" Award in 1997. But the Joy family put it up for sale in 2013, and funding via the Lovington Economic Development Corporation, the City of Lovington and the Local Economic Development Act allowed for the purchase of the theatre in 2014. The Lea Theater is listed in the National Register of Historic Places. It is operated today by the Lea Community Foundation for the Arts.

Jim Harris, the director of the Lea County Museum, contacted me to share some information on another lost theatre located in Lovington: the Aztec Theater (or *Teatro Azteca*), which showed Spanish-language films from the 1950s to the 1970s. An article he wrote shared some information about this sadly forgotten place and about Rosa Trujillo, who at sixteen worked the ticket booth and concessions in the theatre, owned by B.F. "Andy" Moore, who apparently ran a tight ship. He was fair but firm, and anyone getting out of line in the old metal building theatre was politely escorted to the door. In his article about Trujillo, who is now the host at the Lea County Museum, Harris wrote:

> *In 1960, the Spanish-speaking community in Lovington included both Americans and Mexicans. Because the eastern side of New Mexico was farm country thousands of Mexican "braceros" flooded into the area in the 1950s under a federal works program that gave Mexican citizens permits to work in farm regions in several states. There was much work in Texas (just a few miles east), and as a work force and as a cultural force they moved on from South Texas and West Texas into several areas of New Mexico.*
>
> *Rosa, like hundreds of others in Lea County, was an American, having been born and raised in Brownsville, Tex. In many of their customs and*

> *traits, the bracero families were different from her own Trujillo family, but she spoke Spanish, of course, and she had been a neighbor to Mexicans in Brownsville all her life. She was at home in this theater of people.*

Harris continued:

> *Mike Cayton, who was born in San Antonio but went to high school in Lovington and lives in Bulgaria today, tells me that his father set up the* Teatro Azteca.
>
> *Meredith Smith, who lives in Hobbs, and his S&K Real Estate business partner Mark Kennedy owned the theater in the 1970s until its closing as a theater. When it shut down, the building became a Dean Strickland business called "Four-way Bit and Die," at least that is what Mark recalls.*
>
> *Mark says that Mr. Jose Doporto and his wife, who lived in an adobe home on the north side of the theater, operated the business for several years until its closing.*
>
> *Mark also says that by the time he and Meredith had the theater, crowds had begun to thin out, more and more of the young Hispanics in town interested in seeing English-speaking movies, many of which were in color. In addition, in Lovington there was not the bracero presence which was robust in the 1950s.*

The website Bracero History Archive (braceroarchive.org) noted, "The Bracero Program was created by executive order in 1942 because many growers argued that World War II would bring labor shortages to low-paying agricultural jobs. On August 4, 1942, the United States concluded a temporary intergovernmental agreement for the use of Mexican agricultural labor on United States farms (officially referred to as the Mexican Farm Labor Program), and the influx of legal temporary Mexican workers began."

Other houses of cinema in Lovington are said to have included the Wildcat Drive-In, probably named after the local high school team, which had a thirty-year string of hits from 1955 to 1985 and maxed out at nearly five hundred cars; the Mesa, a five-hundred-seater where once again the two titans of ownership pop up, Griffith and Theater Enterprises, which operated this place from 1940 to 1955; the Yucca Drive-In, which enjoyed twenty years of outdoor entertainment from 1955 to 1975; and the Palace, which is said to have shown hits from 1935 to 1945.

Theater names are interesting. Rex, Bijou, Palace, Airdome and others are used over and over. It seems like the owners/operators stuck to names that may have seemed familiar to audiences rather than calling their movie house "the Jeff" or something equally as unfitting.

I have also noted in my research that "arthouse" theatres, which show more than blockbuster films or pictures with big names attached, are few and far between. Although the Fountain in Mesilla shows only foreign and smaller American films, along with a sprinkling of documentaries, only Santa Fe and Albuquerque have had theatre operations that go beyond the norm.

One last stop in far south-central New Mexico is Tatum, north of Lovington and on the cusp of Texas. Once again, the name of the drive-in matches the high school team name, this being Coyote. The Coyote Drive-In, holding two hundred autos, was in the movie business for about twenty years starting in 1955. Information is rare, so I can't swear to accuracy of the opening and closing dates.

I INTENTIONALLY BYPASSED THE biggest town in the region for a while, since the city of Hobbs, population about forty thousand, was a whirlwind of movie theatres, numbering eleven, perhaps twelve, that have come and gone. One of the first might have been the Fawn Theater, which opened on September 6, 1930, and received sound equipment shortly thereafter. Perhaps a year later, it was renamed the Strand, and in 1932, it became the Rex, which was Hobbs's only movie palace for about three years. Sadly, on May 7, 1936, the Rex and ten other businesses burned to the ground in a huge fire that at the time caused $100,000 in damage.

The Scout opened in 1940, lasting until at least 1954. It could offer seating for nearly 750. It may have had an African American owner, but my research only found brief mentions of this.

Another brief note I found, with nothing to back up the statement, said that all theatres in Hobbs closed during the Depression.

The Rig opened on September 19, 1930, and was a "modern all talking playhouse," wrote the late Max Clampitt, who produced the column "Facts, Fantasy or Fiction" every week for the Hobbs *News-Sun* paper. The first feature shown at the Rig was *Manslaughter*, starring Claudette Colbert and Fredric March. The venue was financed by L.C. Griffith of Griffith Theater Enterprises and designed by Gates Corgan of Consolidated Theatres Inc.

The owners of the Rig also had a unique way of getting people to attend the shows. They had a Model A Ford without doors that would go around the town and pick up people, giving them free transport to the movie house. The Rig's projectors ceased operation in 1955, emptying nearly five hundred seats. According to the website Hobbs History (archived at https://archive.is/yyQwV), it also had a contest to name the theatre, offering "a $10 prize for the best name. The money went to an unnamed person who suggested the 'Rig' as a name."

The Roosevelt also had a large auditorium, offering space for nearly 450 movie fans. It started life as the Ritz, beginning in 1929, and was renamed the Roosevelt in the mid-1930s. It suffered two fires, the first in 1934 that apparently started in the projection booth (no injuries) and another in 1951. That time, it was not rebuilt.

A few years later, the Frontier Theater opened, starting in 1952.

The Broadmoor, located at the Broadmoor Shopping Center, did very well for some years, opening in 1969 as part of the Commonwealth chain. It was described as "an intimate, deluxe, jewel-box theatre" with about four hundred seats. The screen was sold to United Artists in the late 1980s before becoming an Allen Theater property in 1998. Allen closed the movie house in 2005, and it was demolished in 2015 to make room for more parking for the shopping center.

The ingeniously named Reel was another indoor movie house in Hobbs, opening in 1937, and it remained in business until at least 1964. Within, it had some beautiful murals painted, depicting Old West scenes.

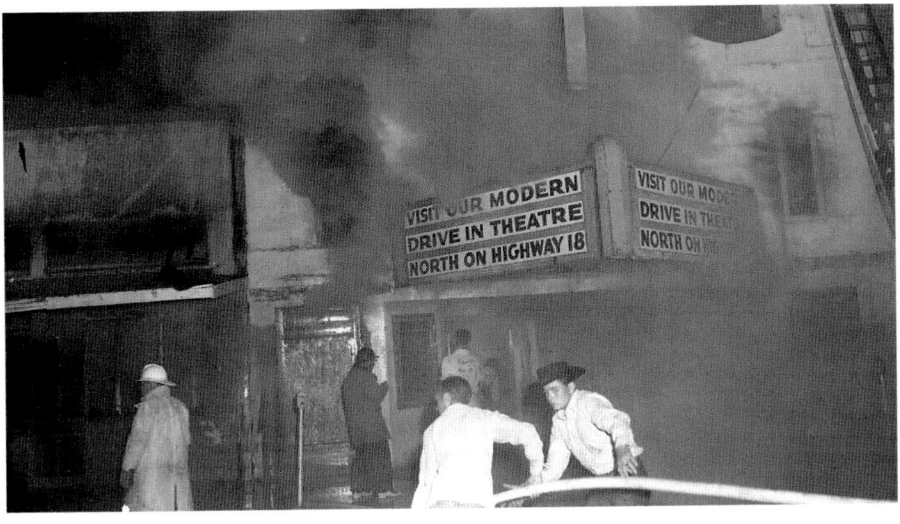

Roosevelt Theater Fire, Hobbs, 1951. *From hobbshistory.com.*

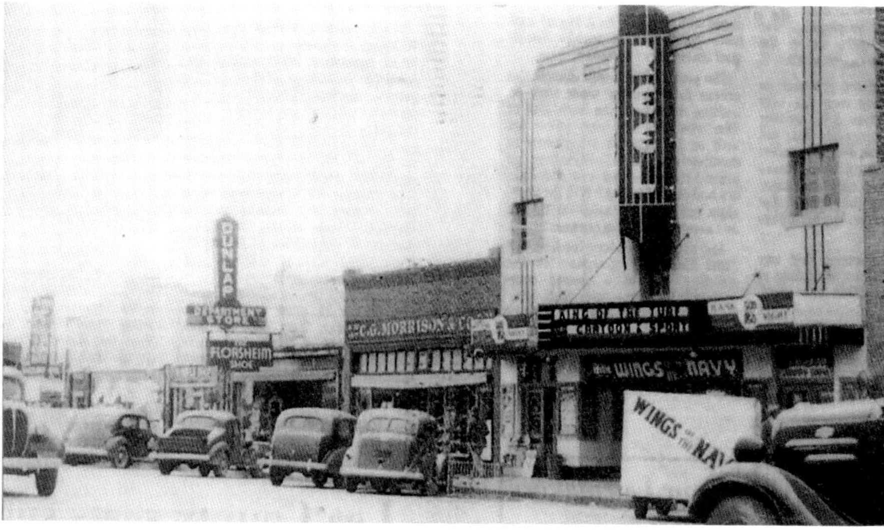

Reel Theater, Hobbs. *From hobbshistory.com.*

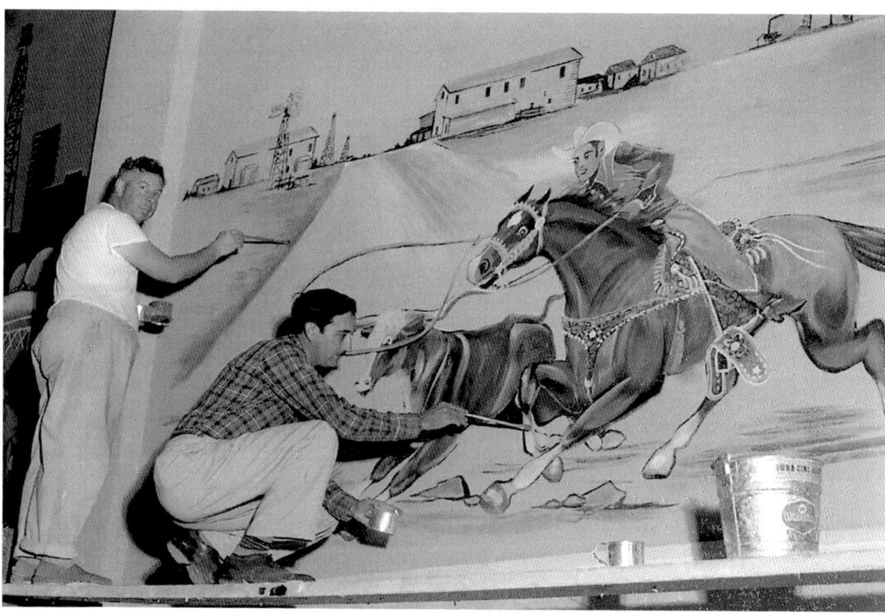

Artist about to be run over by a cowboy! Reel Theater, 1951, Hobbs. *From hobbshistory.com.*

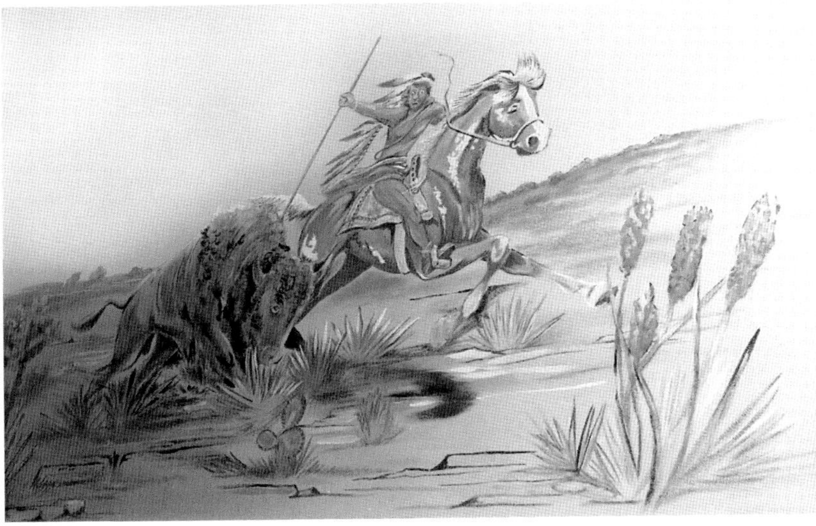

Old West mural, Reel Theater, Hobbs. *From hobbshistory.com.*

The enormous and aptly named Derrick Theater (most of Hobbs's economy is based on oil drilling) became the city's second theatre, according to the Hobbs Public Library. "It was built by Mrs. G.T. Scales of Lubbock (Tex.) and opened for business July 18th, 1930. It opened with a silent film, Sir Rider Haggard's 'Sha.' A live stage show, 'Jazz Jubilee Frolic,' was offered as an added attraction. Admission was 15 and 40 cents." It didn't last long, with the *Film Daily Yearbook* reporting its demise in 1941.

Movies must have been quite the form of entertainment in Hobbs over the years, as so many theatres have opened and closed in the city. Another one from the past is the Eagle Drive-In, which is said to have handled one thousand cars but is now nothing but memories for those who went there to watch movies and/or neck! No pregnancies were reported. It started showing flicks in 1950.

The Flamingo Drive-In, a two-screen affair, could also hold one thousand cars, I have read. It had a great opening in 1955, showing one of the best westerns ever shot in New Mexico, *The Man from Laramie*, which stars Jimmy Stewart and offers New Mexico starring as Wyoming, as does the *Longmire* cable series. The Flamingo's final reels were probably shown in 1985.

With about 750 seats, the Scout opened in 1940 and went through three owners before shutting its doors in 1961.

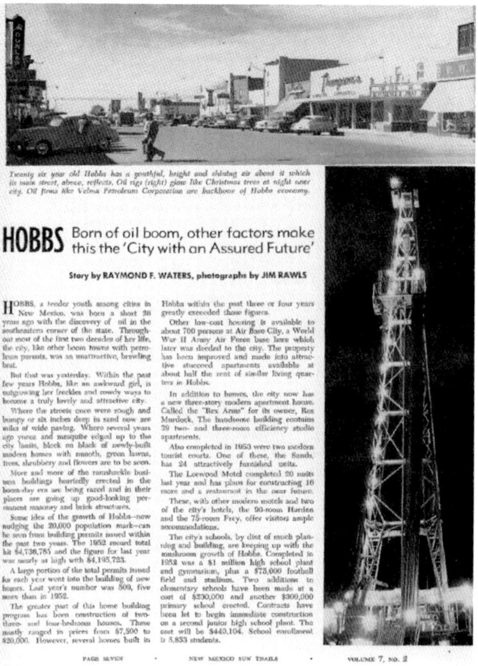

Twenty six year old Hobbs has a youthful, bright and shining air about it which its main street, above, reflects. Oil rigs (right) glow like Christmas trees at night near city. Oil firms like Velma Petroleum Corporation are backbone of Hobbs economy.

HOBBS Born of oil boom, other factors make this the 'City with an Assured Future'

Story by RAYMOND F. WATERS, photographs by JIM RAWLS

HOBBS, a tender youth among cities in New Mexico, was born a short 28 years ago with the discovery of oil in the southeastern corner of the state. Throughout most of the first two decades of her life, the city, like other boom towns with petroleum parents, was an unattractive, brawling brat.

But that was yesterday. Within the past few years Hobbs, like an awkward girl, is outgrowing her freckles and rowdy ways to become a truly lovely and attractive city.

Where the streets once were rough and bumpy or six inches deep in sand now are miles of wide paving. Where several years ago yucca and mesquite edged up to the city limits, block on block of newly-built modern homes with smooth, green lawns, trees, shrubbery and flowers are to be seen.

More and more of the ramshackle business buildings hurriedly erected in the boom-day era are being razed and in their places are going up good-looking permanent masonry and brick structures.

Some idea of the growth of Hobbs—now nudging the 20,000 population mark—can be seen from building permits issued within the past two years. The 1952 record total hit $4,736,785 and the figure for last year was nearly as high with $4,195,723.

A large portion of the total permits issued for each year went into the building of new homes. Last year's number was 509, five more than in 1952.

The greater part of this home building program has been construction of two-, three- and four-bedroom houses. These mostly ranged in prices from $7,500 to $20,000. However, several homes built in Hobbs within the past three or four years greatly exceeded those figures.

Other low-cost housing is available to about 700 persons at Air Base City, a World War II Army Air Force base here which later was deeded to the city. The property has been improved and made into attractive stuccoed apartments available at about half the rent of similar living quarters in Hobbs.

In addition to homes, the city now has a new three-story modern apartment house. Called the "Rex Arms" for its owner, Rex Murdock. The handsome building contains 29 two- and three-room efficiency studio apartments.

Also completed in 1953 were two modern tourist courts. One of these, the Sands, has 24 attractively furnished units.

The Leewood Motel completed 20 units last year and has plans for constructing 16 more and a restaurant in the near future.

These, with other modern motels and two of the city's hotels, the 90-room Harden and the 75-room Frey, offer visitors ample accommodations.

The city's schools, by dint of much planning and building, are keeping up with the mushroom growth of Hobbs. Completed in 1952 was a $1 million high school plant and gymnasium, plus a $75,000 football field and stadium. Two additions to elementary schools have been made at a cost of $230,000 and another $300,000 primary school erected. Contracts have been let to begin immediate construction on a second junior high school plant. The cost will be $440,104. School enrollment is 5,853 students.

PAGE SEVEN • NEW MEXICO SUN TRAILS • VOLUME 7, NO. 2

Left: Article about Hobbs Rig Theater (*on the right*). *From* New Mexico Sun Trails Magazine, *1954*.

Below: Flamingo Drive-In, Hobbs. *From drive-ins.com, Marvin Burrows.*

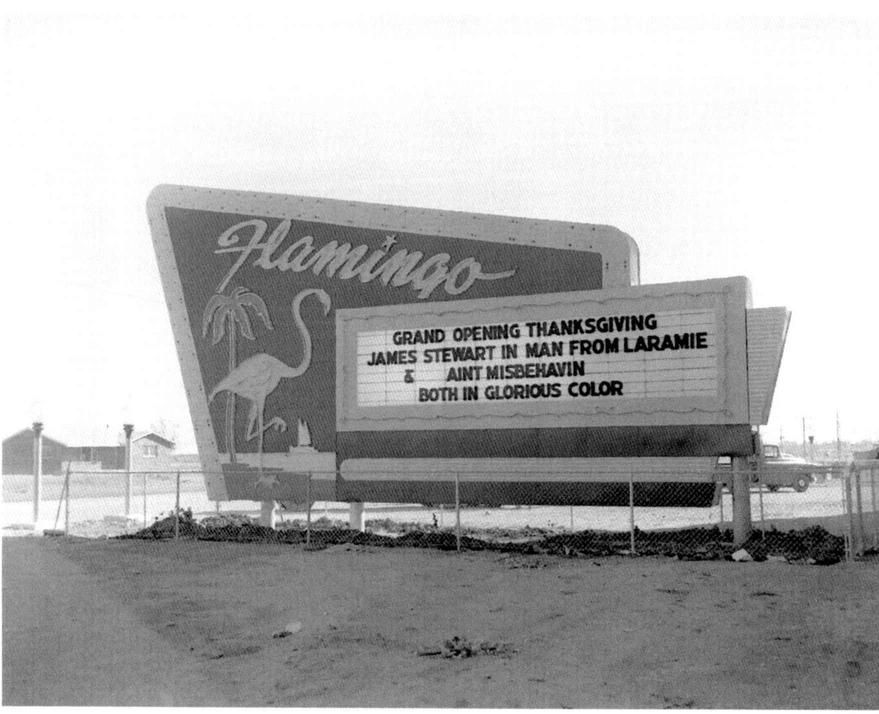

The Sky Vu was the town's first drive-in, opening in 1948 for 350 cars. By 1955, it had been sold to Frontier Theaters by Theater Enterprises. But it is long gone, closing date unknown.

Still another drive-in tried to make its way in Hobbs: the Trade Wind, which opened in 1954, hosting more than five hundred vehicles. Detailed research does not reveal a closing date, other than the theatre was demolished at some point. It was Hobbs's third drive-in. The owner was O.O. Knotts of nearby Eunice, who also owned the Star Drive in that community.

Heading northwest from Hobbs toward Roswell, a few small communities are along the way, including Dexter and Hagerman, each of which had a theatre at one time. The Dexter, in Dexter, might have been in operation in the mid-1950s and had 225 seats, but other data is hard to find.

Hagerman, a town of about 1,200, was once known as Felix and may have had a theatre of the same name at one time. Two other names of theatres are featured on the Cinema Treasures website, the Crystal and Universal, but neither listing has any details.

UNIDENTIFIED FILM OBJECTS

Our long trip has finally brought us to Roswell, New Mexico, the biggest city in the southeast quarter of the state. Since so many theatres have tried to make a go of it in the city, I will only discuss in detail a few that have more than passing details.

As many people know, Roswell is best known for the alleged "crash" of an unidentified flying object (UFO) nearby. Here are some facts you probably don't want to know. It was actually seventy-five miles from Roswell, not "near" Roswell. It was discovered by a cowboy named Mac Brazel (whose uncle, Jesse Wayne Brazel, confessed in 1908 to shooting famed sheriff Pat Garrett, who had shot Billy the Kid), who "found something unusual in his sheep pasture: a mess of metallic sticks held together with tape; chunks of plastic and foil reflectors; and scraps of a heavy, glossy, paper-like material."

Now if that sounds like UFO material to you, I have a nice old movie theatre to sell you. Brazel "hid the material under a bush," and from that, everything from government coverups to UFO corpses—in child-size coffins, no less—has evolved.

Part of the scenario in Roswell that evolved from the "crash" takes place in the former Plains Theatre, a 1,032-seat affair that opened in 1947, closing perhaps in the late 1970s; it is now the UFO Museum and Research Center. The small area near the projection booth offered thirty or so seats for "the exclusive use of Negro patrons." There is contradictory information on this, as other sources note that said seating was in the balcony of the Yucca Theatre.

I find this a bit odd, since just thirty or so years earlier, the settlement of Blackdom was located just a few miles south of Roswell. One of a string of communities founded after the Civil War, Blackdom was for African Americans only and thrived for some years, from about 1903 until the mid-1920s, when a drought and lack of groundwater doomed the small farming community. At one time, it boasted a post office, a school, a newspaper and a store, and few, if any, incidents occurred between the white and black populations. In 1927, Lucy Henderson, a Blackdom resident, wrote to the *Chicago Defender*, a black newspaper, "Here the black man has an equal chance with the white man. Here you are reckoned at the value which you place upon yourself. Your future is in your own hands."

Blackdom was founded by Francis Marion Boyer, who walked from Georgia to New Mexico and then settled in Vado, a small community south of Las Cruces. African American cowboys also founded a small train stop–style village in Dora in northeast New Mexico, which is long abandoned and not related to the town of the same name near Clovis, New Mexico.

Blackdom never sported a cinema. The Plains was the main theatre in Roswell and was state of the art for the times, offering Cinemascope, which was a new addition to the world of film projection. But it was certainly not the only theatre in town. One spot that came and went over the years was the Yucca, which opened in April 1931 with seating for more than nine hundred guests (but no outer space travelers). Once again, the big players were involved, Griffith Amusement Company being the operator. The theatre, now demolished, was open until at least 1963, but historical records are sketchy after that.

The Yucca did get a bit of unique publicity in April 1937 when it went to court over a "lottery device." As indicated by a post on Cinema Treasures, Ken C. McIntyre noted:

> *Appellees were charged with violating Ordinance 397, Section 3, of the Municipal Ordinances of Roswell, in permitting a lottery device to be conducted in the place of business operated by the appellees. The place of business is the Yucca Theatre, owned by R.C. Griffiths Theatres, Inc., and the alleged lottery device is what is commonly known as "Bank Night." In the police magistrate's court the appellees were found guilty and fined $25 each. They appealed to the district court where the cause was tried de novo. The district court ruled that:*

> *The device complained of does not constitute a lottery device in that the participants in "Bank Night" pay nothing to either register or participate in the drawing, it being equally free to those who do not even purchase a ticket as to those who do purchase a ticket, there being no consideration for the chance to win, and as a conclusion the court finds no violation of the ordinance.*
>
> *The court discharged the appellees, dismissed the complaint, and the City of Roswell prosecutes this appeal from such judgment. The Attorney General enters his appearance amicus curiae in support of the City of Roswell.*
>
> *The spirit of gambling, the squandering of savings, the evils aimed at by our lottery statute, can no more be found in "Bank Night" than can be found in the numerous advertising schemes seen daily where thousands of dollars are given away as prizes to "slogan coiners" or "lucky guessers" who send to the manufacturer a wrapper from a can of soup or bar of soap.*
>
> *Although signing one's name in a book or appearing at the theatre within five minutes of the time of the drawing might be regarded as consideration, it cannot be called "pay" without warping the word out of all recognition. It clearly is not a game of hazard in which small sums of money are ventured for the chance of obtaining a larger value in money or other articles.*
>
> *For the reasons given, the judgment of the trial court will be sustained. It is so ordered.*

Indeed.

Another name from the past is the Princess Theatre, which opened in Roswell in July 1913, was renamed the Liberty and was renamed again in about 1940 to the Pecos Theater. The site accommodated 725 and had room for a three-piece orchestra. The building has since been demolished. Originally, it was operated by K&F Amusement Company of Colorado.

In more modern times, the Cinema 4 became part of Roswell's economic base in May 1984. By 1990, the screens had been sold three times, and it was finally shut down by the last owner, Allen Theatres, in 2006, when that chain opened an eight-screen multiplex nearby.

The Chief, another movie palace built for audiences of the day, seated seven hundred patrons and probably operated from 1950 to 1964.

Roswell is also home to the New Mexico Military Institute, which had its own theatre(s) years ago, the Broncho and Pearson Auditorium.

The El Capitan was originally opened by someone other than Griffith. The Civic Theater Company operated this theatre starting in 1925. Its five hundred seats were permanently empty by 1950. The Majestic showed silent films in 1907, including *All Aboard* and *Train Wreckers*, which were deemed "worth the price of admission." The newspaper of the day offered, "Go and have a hearty laugh. It will do you good." The Majestic might have also been the Capital Theatre, which could hold four hundred patrons and was open before 1908. The Park Twin and Del Norte Twin were also owned by Allen Theatres but were both closed when the New Mexico–based theatre corporation opened the Galaxy 8 in 2006.

A plethora of drive-ins also dotted the landscape around Roswell—two with very interesting names, the Ball-O-Jak and the Jingle Bob. The Ball-O-Jak sported a single screen for five hundred autos and was opened in the early 1950s, perhaps 1953. It was finished showing flickers by 1980 and changed hands twice after its opening by Theater Enterprises, with Commonwealth Theatres being the final proprietor. There's no explanation as to why it had that name, but I wonder if it was the name of a local cattle ranch.

The Jingle Bob was somewhat smaller, offering three hundred car spaces. It also had the same three owners during its boom years, 1955–69. And in case you have never lived on a ranch, a jingle bob has two meanings, I discovered. One I knew about, which is that it is a part of a spur that makes noise when a cowperson is walking about, kind of like chimes on spurs on boots. It can also be "a cattle marking consisting of an ear slashed so that the halves dangle beside the head." Ouch.

The other cinemas listed for this fair city include the Yucca Drive-In; the El Cortez (or Cortez) indoor venue, which had about 500 chairs but only lasted about ten years from the mid-1940s to the mid-1950s; and the Starlite (or Star-Lite or Starlight) Drive-In, which also opened during the heyday of drive-in movies, around 1955, and later added a second screen. That expansion allowed for almost 1,100 carriages to sit under the stars, at least through 1960 and perhaps as late as 1985.

The Star-Lite had the claim to fame in 1947, before it was even open, of having three UFOs being sighted over it by a security patrol at the Roswell Army Air Field, who reported, "The UFO's were headed straight to the air field. At 21:30 all 3 UFO's came across the air field. At that time troops opened fire with antiaircraft guns. 2 of the UFO's evaded the fire and disappeared from site. The 3rd UFO was struck and began to shoot flames from the area hit. The injured ship headed back toward the edge of town. It went across 6 mill hill and crash landed in a field." Spare me….

The Drive-In Theater website noted that Project Silver Screen was begun in 1948 "to study the connection between the large number of Drive-In Theaters being built and the growing number of UFOsiteings [*sic*] around them. The data showed that the Aliens some how [*sic*] controlled where the Drive-In would be built." Ahem. You know it must be true since it's on the Internet!

Let's zoom away from Roswell now and head for some small communities to the north and east before we land in the cities of Portales and Clovis.

LAND OF THE PEANUT FARMS

Elida, which now has fewer than two hundred residents, is just southwest of the two bigger communities noted. It was home to a movie house, the Apache Theatre, which according to Bryan Krefft on Cinema Treasures "opened in 1946 in a building that formerly housed a roller-skating rink. The movie theater was short-lived and closed in 1955."

Just a smidge farther up the road is Kermit (not named after the famed frog), which was once called Plateau, but whatever the name, it no longer exists. Allegedly when it did, the Kermit Theater was part of the village, in about 1950. However, I can find no historical reference to the place.

Here we'll take a side trip to the villages of Melrose and Fort Sumner before tackling the numerous venues that once existed in Portales and Clovis. Melrose did have the 225-seat Rialto Theater, which was opened before World War II, perhaps in 1940, before the lights went out in 1955. It is interesting and sad that there is not more information about these tiny town venues. Part of what I found on the Rialto was from the obituary of a lady who worked there, who met her future husband at the moving picture show.

Fort Sumner is most famed for its alleged grave of the famed Billy the Kid (although I have read that the graves and contents washed away in a flood years ago), after he was shot by Sheriff Pat Garrett, as well as its connection to the Long Walk, which took place from 1864 to 1866, when the Dine (Navajo) people were forced from their traditional desert lands to the high, dry plains of eastern New Mexico. The town is also home, I think, to the Dazend Movie Museum, which never answers its phone.

Three theatres may have roots in the community, with only the Zia being a sure bet. It still stands and is covered by a colorful mural. At one time, it was owned by Helene Haack and John Allen and may have operated prior to 1945 until 1950. Upon the passing of her husband in 1945, Ms. Allen successfully ran the family businesses before passing away in 1978.

There is also brief mention of the Granada Theater, but the only readily available detail on this business is a live boxing match around 1933 in which local hero Joe Perry "clobbered" "Texaco Rambler" in a mere forty seconds, while his seventeen-year-old brother, Jim, decked Vernon Baker. Both went on to local fame in their profession, and it appears that Fort Sumner once produced a number of worthy boxers in the 1930s.

Now arriving in Portales, a place the grows great peanuts, we find that, oddly, the town that is home to a university, Eastern New Mexico University, and has a non-ENMU population of thirteen thousand has no movie theatre. Instead, the population must go twenty miles to Portales for a multiplex run by Allen Theatres. Such has not always been the case, and there is hope that the Yam will once again start showing movies. The once-upon-a-time five-hundred-seat movie house, according to Portales MainStreet (portalesmainstreet.org), has this history:

> *In the 1920s America experienced a building boom of "movie palaces." The "Portola Theater" opened in August 1926 and was billed as one of the most up-to-date motion picture theatres in the State of New Mexico, offering comfortable seating and modern organ music with a large stage.*
>
> *In 1929, the "Portola Theater" became the "Palace Theater." With the on-set of the Great Depression in 1929, there was a severe decline in theatre attendance across the nation and unfortunately the "Palace Theater" became a statistic and closed its doors.*
>
> *In 1932, the "Palace Theater" was purchased, reopened and renamed "The Portola." Later that year the theatre was renovated and given a new name "The Yam," taking its name from the major agricultural crop produced in Roosevelt County at the time, sweet potatoes. It remained a working theatre and retained the name "The Yam" until circa 1963–1965 when it once again closed its doors.*
>
> *In 2002, through a private donation from Addie Peed Swearingen, the theatre was purchased by the Portales MainStreet Program. Thanks to additional donations, fundraising and many state and federal grants, the City of Portales and the Portales MainStreet Program have been able to completely renovate the theatre.*

> *Today the facility includes a meeting room, lobby, ticket booth, dressing room, bathrooms, concession area, projection booth and large multi-use theater space.*

Sadly, there was a negative post recently about the venue during an event, where the guest rattled on about no heat, cooling or air circulation, so the renovation may need to continue. An anonymous donor ponied up $100,000 in 2003 as seed money to start the purchase of the building. Once used as a warehouse, the Yam was deeded to the City of Portales to continue funding the makeover.

Other houses of celluloid that once operated in Portales included the Kiva, which fell in line with the usual aspects of a Griffith Amusement Company venue—four hundred or so seats, opening in 1940 and selling in '45 to Theatre Enterprises, which closed the venue in 1955.

Rupert Earl Griffith was an interesting character. Old records dating back to 1915 show that Rupert Earl and his two brothers, Louis Clyde and Henry Jefferson, purchased their first theatre in San Marcos, Texas. By 1936, they had interests in 125 theatres in fifty-eight communities and had eighty partners via the Griffith Amusement Company and Griffith Consolidated Theaters.

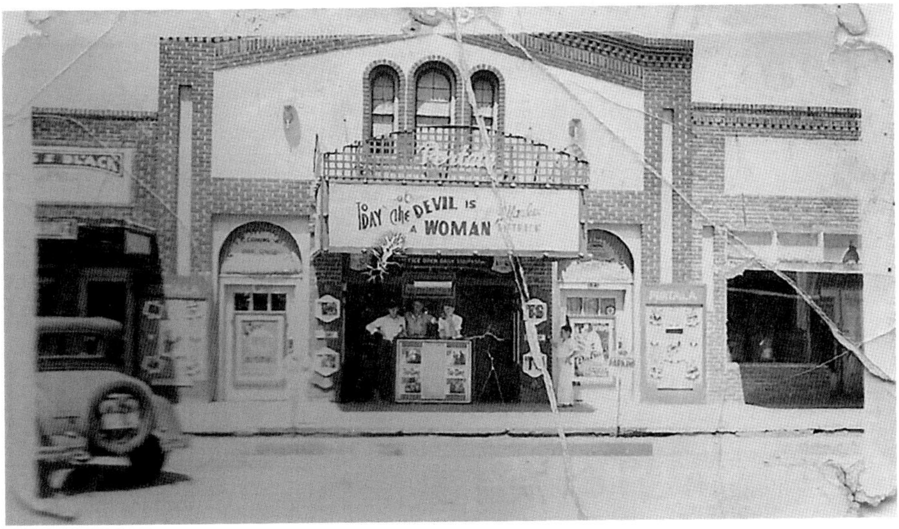

Portola Theater, later the Yam, Portales. *Portales Main Street.*

In 1949, eight employees, led by company attorney Henry S. Griffing, bought the Griffith stock and formed Video Independent Theatres. By 1951, Video was running 157 screens in forty-eight towns, including 42 drive-in theatres. They acquired numerous other movie houses, numbering nearly 800 before R.E. reached the age of fifty. His business acumen branched into the hotel business, and he built the famed El Rancho Motel in Gallup, New Mexico. Besides New Mexico, the theatre holdings branched out into Missouri, Texas, Arkansas, Oklahoma, Arizona, Kansas and Nebraska.

Sadly, R.E. passed away in 1943. The Griffith stock was sold in 1949 to eight of Griffith employees, who formed Video Independent Theatres. And contrary to the story of many years, R.E. Griffith was not the brother of famed film director D.W. Griffith, although he claimed as much for many years.

Liberty, Lyric, Tower, Crawley's Drive-In and Varsity Drive-In were also venues that failed in Portales. Crawley's, now the site of a church, was capable of handling two hundred vehicles. Operating in the zenith of drive-ins, Crawley's has little history noted but seemingly operated in the mid-1950s under the direction of Perry Crawley.

Originally a single-screen movie house, the Tower Twin was shut down in June 2009 when the air conditioning system failed. The cost of replacing it made it unfeasible to reopen, and it now sits idle, although in 2015, the current owner said he was going remodel it (though not as a movie theatre). We await.

The original Tower Theatre opened in 1950 with more than nine hundred seats. The building burned in 1978 and was rebuilt as a twin-screen hall at that time. It went through several more owners before being purchased in 1990 by Allen Theatres, which today owns most of the venues in smaller and midsized towns across the state.

The Liberty and Lyric may have existed during those boom years in the 1950s, with the Liberty offering up 350 seats, but no further information is readily available.

Clovis, a city of about forty thousand just twenty minutes from Portales, has also offered its friendly confines to numerous movie proprietors over the years. It has one of the most interesting theatre histories in the entire state. Clovis was founded in 1907, and in those days, it served as a railroad siding and a center for ranching and farming. The downtown area began to grow, and it wasn't long before two theatres appeared, the Clovis Grand and the Unigus. Two more theatres appeared in the early years, including the Grand and the Airdome, an open-air theatre.

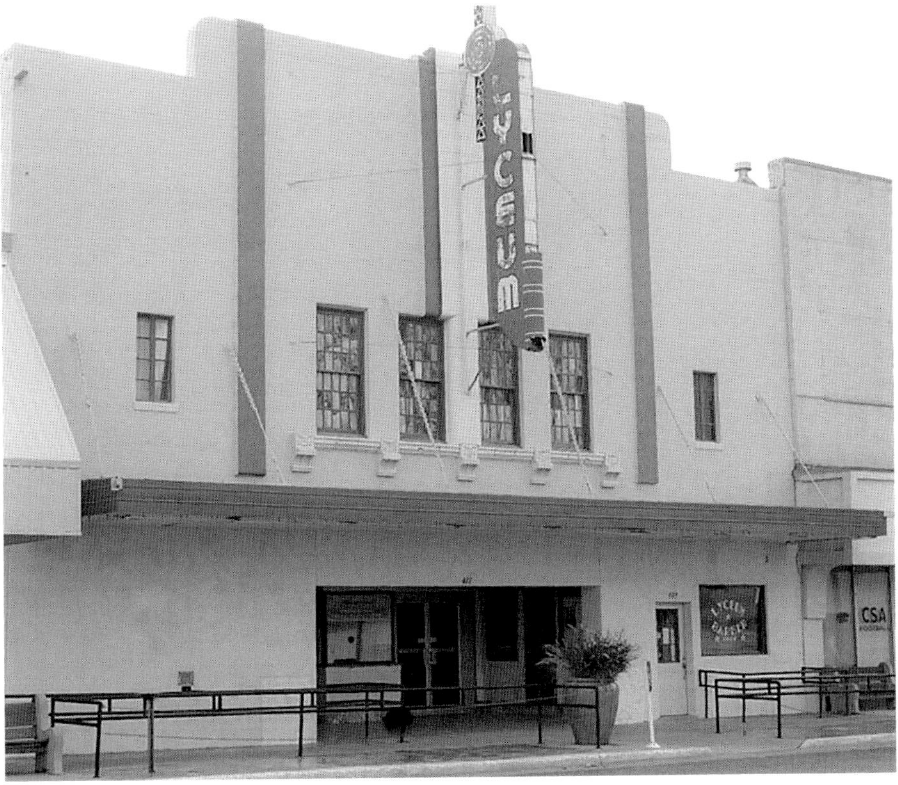

Lyceum Theater, Clovis. *Wikimedia Commons, cspear.*

Dr. David Kammer's research finds that these movie houses "soon offered over a thousand feet of movie film as well as slide shows with musical accompaniment nightly. Initially, children paid a nickel and adults a dime to attend an evening's entertainment." Probably the most notable is the Lyceum, which opened in 1912, built for Eugene F. Hardwick for vaudeville production and movies. It, like many New Mexico movie houses, is built in the style of a Spanish mission.

Hardwick sold his ranch and moved to Clovis. In 1915, he built a twenty-five-foot arch across Main Street in front of the Lyceum Theatre.

In 1929, the Lyceum offered its very first "talking picture" in 1929, *Chinatown Nights* with Wallace Beery. The auditorium also saw personal appearances by the renowned John Philip Sousa, Gene Autry, Will Rogers, silent film cowboy star Tom Mix (who once had a studio in Las Vegas, New Mexico) and Shirley Temple.

The Lyceum held six hundred or nine hundred (depending on what source you believe), was air conditioned, was "retired" in 1974 and was acquired by the city in 1982. According to the CinemaTour website, the Hardwicks opened the State Theatre just down the street from the Lyceum in January 1940.

The State "is considered the most striking example of modernism found in any New Mexico theatre. A circular glass-block tower rises from above the marquee and reaches higher than the curved parapet that masks a barrel roof. Its modern air-conditioning system and fresh style inspired the Hardwicks to restyle the Lyceum's exterior, giving it a molded stucco façade in the Streamline Moderne style. The Hardwicks kept up to date and retained a competitive edge over theater chains that started to move into Clovis at the time." The Hardwicks became an affiliate of good ol' Griffith in 1933. The State went through the now typical string of owners—Commonwealth, Frontier and United Artists—before shutting down in about 1987.

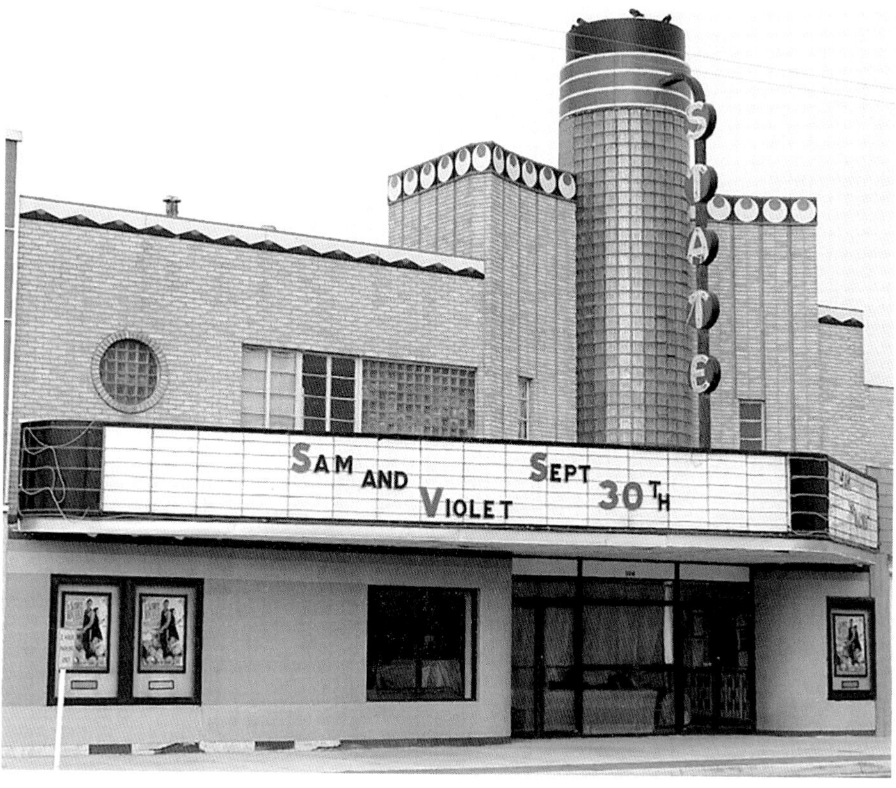

State Theatre, Clovis. *Wikimedia Commons.*

Playwright Robert Patrick—who once lived in eastern New Mexico and worked as an usher, ticket-taker and concession hand at four Roswell theatres—recalled some memories of the Lyceum and State on his blog:

> *The State with its still-famous and still-standing "tower" sign was the grade-a-number-one theatre. The State got the M.G.M., Twentieth Century Fox, Warner Brothers, and Walt Disney pictures. It was where one took "nice girls" for dates. The elite of Junior High School, the "Popcorn Gang," always went together to the State.*
>
> *The Lyceum, across Main Street from the Sunshine, was in the early 1950s the "kids' theatre" of Clovis, playing double bills of shoot-'em-up westerns, car-chase cop movies, and wacky kid-comedies. The Lyceum also occasionally played first-run, "A" movies that were not considered quite right for the State or the Sunshine.*

The Sunshine, an independent theatre, is a rarity from the past. It opened in Clovis on May 30, 1941, and saw its sun set for good in 1954. It was owned and operated by Lloyd Franklin, who went to work for the Yucca Drive-In after the closing of the Sunshine, which even sported 3-D. It was another grand-sized theatre, with five hundred to six hundred seats.

Mesa is a popular name for movie theatres in New Mexico, and Clovis has had several of them over the years. The first Mesa opened during the silent era, showing its first picture show sometime in 1918. It was in competition with the Lyceum until the owners of that operation bought out the Mesa owner in the 1920s.

Seating almost one thousand patrons, the second Mesa was opened with architecture by E.C. Parker after the first Mesa burned down. It was built on the same lot as the original, this time for our friends at Griffith Theatres. Its first screenings, on August 26, 1931, were sold-out showings of *I Take This Woman*, starring Gary Cooper and Carole Lombard.

It, too, burned in 1948, and it is thought that the exterior walls survived the disaster. Reconstruction began on March 6, 1948, with owner E.R. Hardwick stating that "everything in the theater would be new, including the four [segregated] rest rooms." The stadium-style auditorium was to seat 768. The architect for the project was Jack Corgan, and it reopened on December 29, 1948, with *Deep Waters*, starring Jean Peters and Dana Andrews.

By October 1960, the theatre, which was only open two days a week by then, went to showing only Spanish-language movies. Its last screening was on November 20, 1960, with *Dos Maridos Baratos* (*Two Cheap Husbands*), a comedy-western.

The final Mesa was purchased that same year by music producers Norman and Vi Petty, whose studio in Clovis was where Buddy Holly, Waylon Jennings and Roy Orbison once cut recordings. It is no longer a cinema but rather was converted to "a fully equipped and acoustically advanced radio station, recording studio and performance auditorium" and is now owned by Zia Broadcasting.

Robert Patrick also remembered this cinematic paradise very well on his blog:

> *The Mesa was just across the street from the Hotel Clovis, right by the railroad tracks, and was tacitly thought of as a diversion "for transients," which would include traveling salesmen, land—or cattle—buyers, military personnel* [Cannon Air Base is in this area], *migratory workers, and the like. One could pick up illegal whisky at the Mesa. "That end of town" was thought of as slightly sleazy, although it can't have been more than five blocks from the shiny intersection of Main and Seventh Streets, where the Courthouse and the First Methodist Church.*
>
> *On those rare occasions when an "adult" movie was allowed to slip into town, it played the Mesa. My brother-in-law took me there with him to see a movie of strip-tease dancers. The performers never got farther down than to pasties and bikinis, which rankled my brother-in-law. He said that usually when he went to see such movies there, they showed whole breasts.*
>
> *An exception to the rule that adult movies played the Mesa was a "roadshow" called "Mom and Dad," a sort of negative instructional drama about teenage pregnancy, which played at the Lyceum. There were separate showings for boys only and girls only.*

Clovis also had a Plains Theatre, again owned by the Hardwicks. A note on the Cinema Treasures site offered that "E. Russell Hardwick of the Lyceum, State and Mesa theaters went with a 450-seat [it may have been 360] theater in the 200 block of South Main. Long gone and unsuccessful, the Plains launched March 12, 1937 with 'The Plainsman' [starring Gary Cooper]....It closed throughout World War II due to personnel shortages, reopened on December 29, 1945 for just two days a week, [but] it didn't work out."

A more recent effort was the Hilltop Twin, owned and operated by Commonwealth Theatres. The five-hundred-seat emporium of celluloid had a grand opening on October 5, 1973. In May 1986, Commonwealth

Theatres was sold to the Cannon Group, and it retained Commonwealth name. At one time, the Cannon Group was one of Europe's largest exhibitors. Commonwealth operated 425 screens in twelve states then.

In 1989, Cannon/Commonwealth sold the Hilltop Twin to United Artists Theatres, which sold it a year later to Allen Theatres, which operated it until June 2006, closing it due to meager attendance. It is now an early learning center called Future Generations.

In 1940, there may have been an operation called the Clovis Theatre owned by Griffith, but no other evidence of this could be found.

Drive-ins in Clovis were numerous as well, with the Yucca, La Fonda, Comet and Four Lane all vying for business at one time or another. The La Fonda's first feature was the 1951 Foreign Legion movie *Ten Tall Men*, starring Burt Lancaster. The release of that movie is listed as October 1951, but an old ad for the theatre noted that the grand opening was on the Fourth of July. I would believe the ad. The La Fonda was first operated by Lloyd Franklin, but upon its closing in 1985, after it had expanded to two screens, Commonwealth was operating it.

Lloyd Franklin also operated the Yucca, which opened in the summer of 1948 hosting 350 cars. No reports could be found of how many scalawags snuck in while hiding in trunks. It stayed in business until 1980. It is now demolished, with homes having been built on the property.

Information on the Four Lane is as rare as operating a drive-in.

The Four Lane was opened in 1954, as an ad from the *Clovis News-Journal* stated that the site was showing a great film noir–type movie, *Riot in Cell Block 11*. The only other information on this passion pit is that it might have ended its run in 1964 and had parking for 350 vehicles.

Even less information is available for the Comet, which has a very cool name. An old newspaper ad shows that it was open in April 1960, but this will need more research.

Onward.

THE HI LO COUNTRY

Our next stops will be in the northeast corner of the Land of Enchantment. It is a beautiful but sparsely populated area, with most economic development coming from ranching. It is called the Hi Lo Country, a phrase coined by author Max Evans, who cowboyed in this area for many years and wrote the book of the same name based on his experience as a cow puncher before and after World War II. The book was made into a movie in 1998, shot in the area, and it's one of the finest movies ever made in and about New Mexico.

It was defined and named by Evans himself. "It embraces the northeastern half of New Mexico, the far panhandle of Oklahoma, a lot of southeastern Colorado, and extends over into the far northwest of Texas." Charles Champlin, the late *Los Angeles Times* writer and film critic, called the area "a difficult, dry, testing land, a mix of mountains and wide plains, all wind-swept." And that might be what happened to many of the movie palaces, large and small, that once dotted this area.

Along Interstate 40, which parallels and is related to historic US 66, there are the towns of San Jon, Tucumcari and Santa Rosa. San Jon (pronounced "san hone"), which has an elevation of 4,032 feet above sea level, had a population of about two hundred in 2013. It is not too far from the Texas border, and prior to the opening of I-40, it was the largest town in this part of New Mexico. During the glory days of Route 66, it was quite a tourist stop, boasting many motels, gas stations and cafés. After 1981, with I-40 getting more traffic than the soon-to-be-unmaintained 66, San Jon started to fade away.

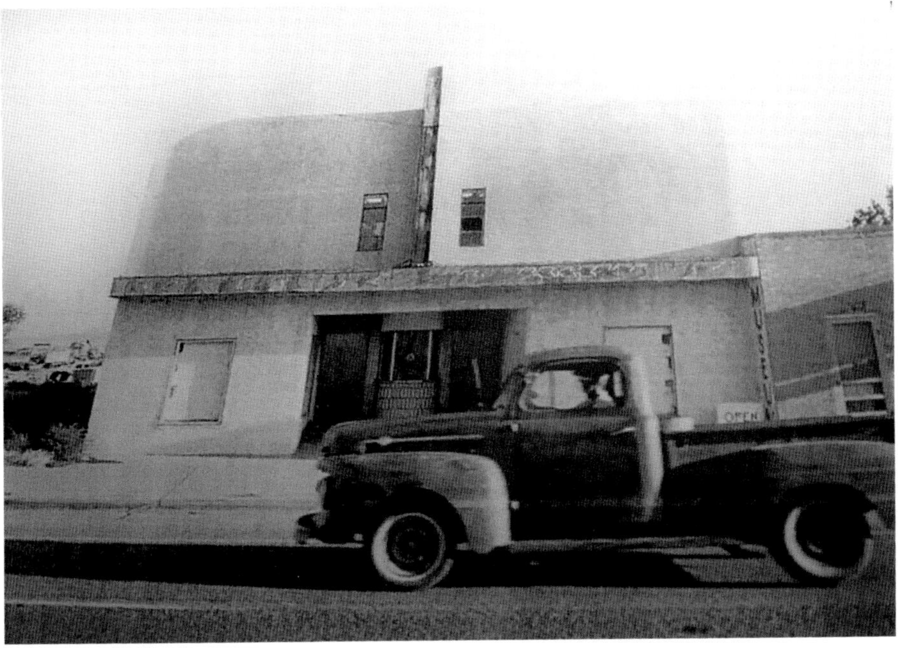

Ute Theater, San Jon. *From sanjon.org*

At one time (year of operation not listed), there is mention of three theatres in the community: the State, which, amazingly, could hold nearly seven hundred; the San Jon; and the Ute. My guess is that there was a theatre, but it changed hands or names several times before fading into obscurity. No matter what its history, it closed long before 1980.

Tucumcari, on the other hand, has taken its Route 66 roots and made itself into an interesting travelers' town, highlighting the history of the "mother road." Arch Hurley had operated the Evans Opera House in Tucumcari until 1915, when he opened the New Theater, which he replaced with the Princess Theater in 1917 after it suffered serious flood damage.

There was also an open-air silent film venue that began business in 1908, the Air Dome. It was also called the H&H, after the two gents who built it, Gene Hawkins and Arch Hurley. Hurley assumed sole ownership in 1921 and changed the name to Princess.

In the fall of 1937, Hurley reopened the renovated and updated Princess with a screening of *Vogues of 1938*, which was nominated for three Academy Awards. As so often happens, the theatre burned, with only the outside shell being saved. This took place in 1943, but Hurley was not deterred. Rather, he rebuilt and updated the movie box again, making it slightly bigger, as it

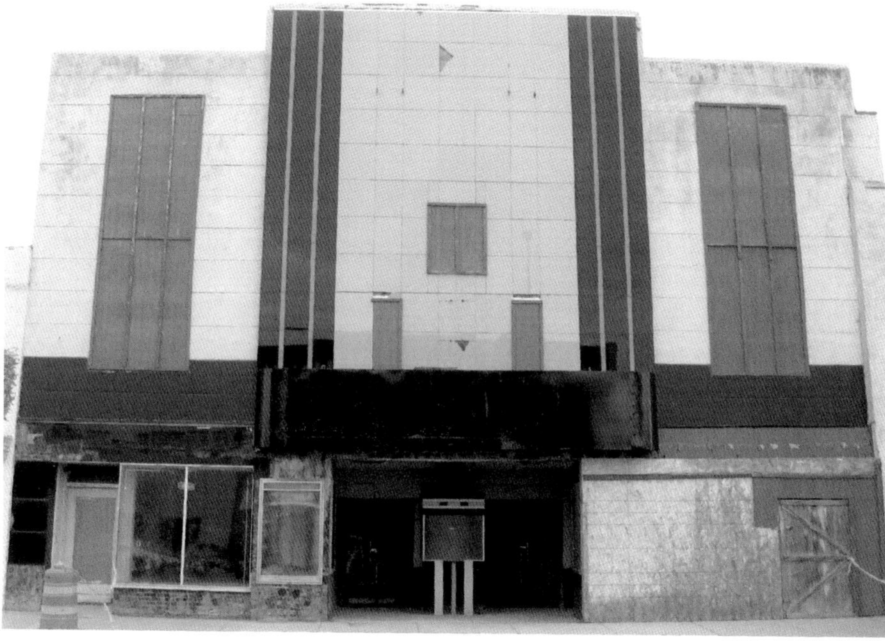

This page: Princess Theatre, Tucumcari. *From Cinema Treasures, contributed by Bill Eichelberger.*

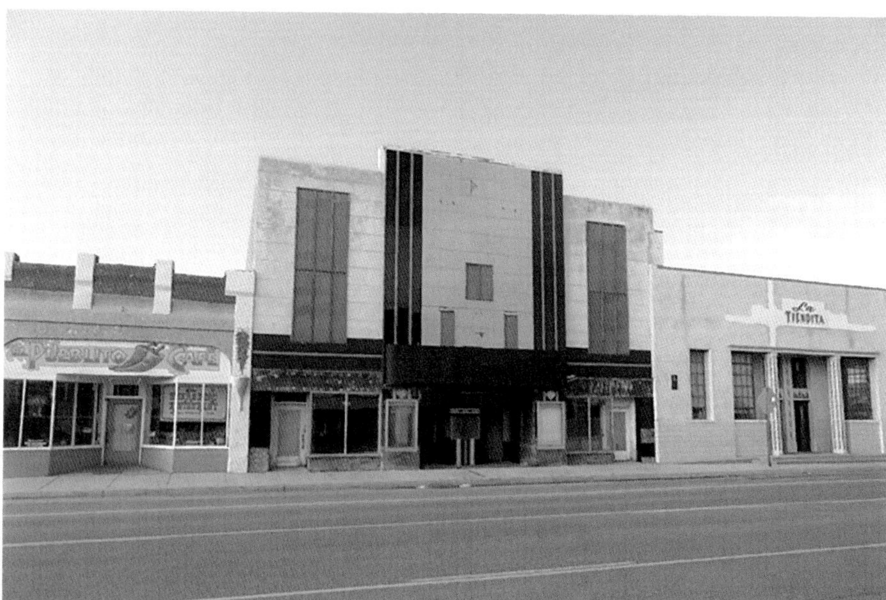

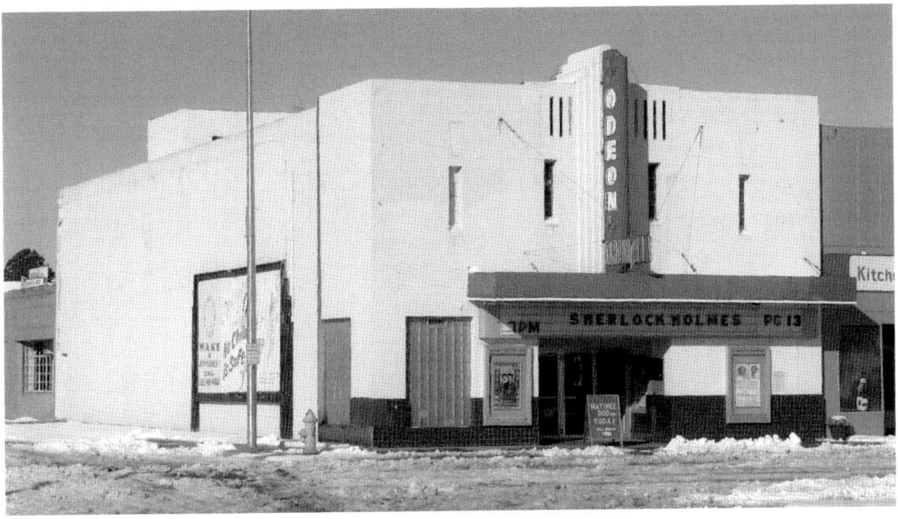

Odeon Theater, Tucumcari. *Wikimedia Commons.*

now seated eight hundred. But good fortune was not on his side, as there was another fire on the roof in 1962. After that, the silver screen bastion was boarded up.

The long-closed seven-hundred-seat Princess is now owned by the Town of Tucumcari, but plans to restore it have yet to come to fruition. Also in Tucumcari, there is a "genuine pre–World War II motion picture theatre with Art Deco details," the Odeon, which took over the space that the Air Dome had a few years earlier.

The Odeon Theater opened on May 16, 1936, apparently under the ownership of Hurley, who "received congratulatory telegrams from movie greats Frank Capra and Mary Astor when it opened." Still in business, the auditorium now seats 385 viewers and the balcony 90, although that might be closed at this writing. The theatre is also in the National Register of Historic Places. Allegedly, as the Greek word *odeon* means "theatre," the name was chosen because "it was short and cheapened the costs of the neon sign."

The Canal Drive-In also operated in this town from at least 1951, when it screened the John Wayne flick *Flying Leathernecks*, to probably 1975, when it was owned by Frontier Theatres. The unusual but unproven thing about this theatre is that it had room for 400 cars but also 250 seats, suggesting that it also allowed for outdoor viewing outside the confines of a cramped auto.

There is also a brief listing for the County Drive-In, of which it can be noted that it was operating in 1960, but other facts aren't on my desk. It may have lasted one more year, when the last of five hundred cars pulled out.

During the Great Depression, the Conchas Dam, some ways north of Tucumcari along the Canadian River, became a New Deal project. Sometime around 1935, after the initial homes and important buildings were finished for the construction town, a startlingly large movie theatre was built, holding seven hundred patrons. At some point, it was operated by Commonwealth Theatres. It, like Conchas, is now mostly memory.

Farther west on I-40 is Santa Rosa, another Route 66 revival town; it once had a movie theatre called the Rodeo. Later renamed the Pecos, the small movie house closed for good in October 2010.

According to the website Route 66 News, "The Pecos Theatre began as the El Paso Tiempo in 1919, then was the Santa Rosa Theatre in 1920, the Kiva in 1951, the Rodeo in 1936, and finally the Pecos in 1981. Except for a nine-month period in 1980, the theater had been operating continuously."

It had 350 seats, and Ira Smith was the original owner. He went on to open a motel some years later. It was purchased by the County of Guadalupe in 2016, which is currently upgrading it with $700,000 in repairs.

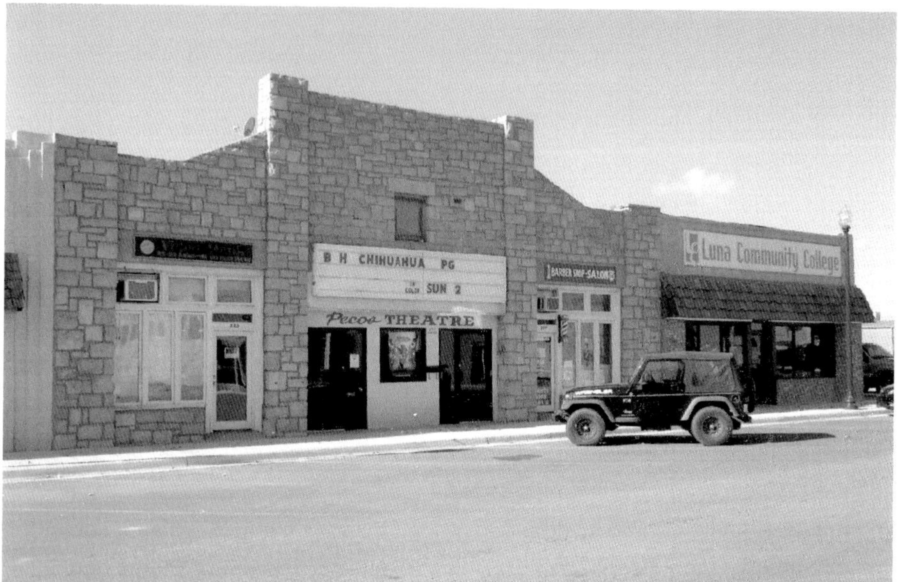

Rodeo/Pecos Theatre, Santa Rosa. Shuttered. *Randy Carlisle.*

The Sky Ranch Drive-In also flourished in Santa Rosa, hosting 250 eager movie seekers from the 1950s to the mid-1970s. A big deal happened here according to the *Santa Rosa News*: on August 29, 1952, the theatre had some unexpected guests. "Joe Pat Downing and Eddie Racel, employees at the Sky-Ranch Drive-in Theater, today reported that they saw a number of triangular-shaped objects circling the skies around Santa Rosa just after midnight last night. The objects reportedly left the area, heading east, and then returned for a repeat performance." Zounds!

Before heading deep into the Hi Lo part of New Mexico, we'll swing a bit southwest-ish to the communities of Vaughn, Estancia, Belen and Mountainair. Stopping first in Vaughn, which in my travels has proven to be one of the saddest-feeling towns in the whole state, there are three theatre listings: Resort, Studio and West. The Studio seems the most likely, as an old newspaper ad for 1960 lists *Battle in Outer Space* as a coming attraction. Operating with three hundred seats, the venue might have been open from 1940 to 1955. But in my calls throughout the community, there is little to indicate any type of theatre building still standing, hence it might be demolished. No other tidbits on either the Resort or West are offered, other than the West may have been screening from 1940 to 1945 and the Resort in 1955. I'm thinking that this was the same theatre, just with a name change.

Mountainair, a pleasant community west of Vaughn, was once called the "Pinto Bean Capital of the World" until a drought struck in the late 1940s. With that moniker, it makes sense that the Pinto Theater was operating during the early 1950s, with vacancy for 450. Prior to that, there are listings for the Quivira in 1935 and the Real from 1940 to 1945 but no details, again suggesting that these were all the same place, just with name changes. The Pinto, owned by Theater Enterprises, closed in 1955.

And now to Estancia to visit the Star Theater, which I almost purchased myself in the early 1990s. The theatre then was still open on occasion, perhaps on weekends, and had a busy sandwich shop next door. The lobby of the theatre was used for seating for the restaurant patrons, and it was a going little enterprise. The seating in the theatre was compact, about 250, and some restoration was in order, along with another real job that would help supplement the business.

My kind and caring wife at the time, Libby, thought we could do it if one or both of us was to be able to transfer with the U.S. Postal Service, where we both worked at the time. I desperately wanted a new career, and her loving support was amazing. She liked her job, a middle management position, and mine was okay, as I was postmaster in the amazing town of Pryor, a tiny community of the Crow Indian Nation in south-central Montana.

We debated back and forth for some time about this decision, which would also include the operation of a small coffeehouse about to open nearby. However, in the end, we opted not to, as the economy of Estancia seemed to be stagnant, with little hope of revival. Later, Libby and I parted ways as well, and I still don't own a movie theatre.

The Star is now closed, as is the sandwich shop, and the theatre is now owned by the Victory Church. The little theatre has been closed for some time after opening in the 1940s and later being operated by Theater Enterprises.

Another great movie made in New Mexico, *White Sands*, was partially shot in Estancia in 1991, as were parts of *Convoy* (1978) and *Hell or High Water* (2016), the latter a finalist for a Best Picture Oscar in 2017. So near and yet so far.

West of Estancia and Mountainair is the town of Belen, located on I-25 about forty minutes south of Albuquerque. Over the last few years, Belen has become a favorite spot for filmmakers to shoot, including the 2016 release

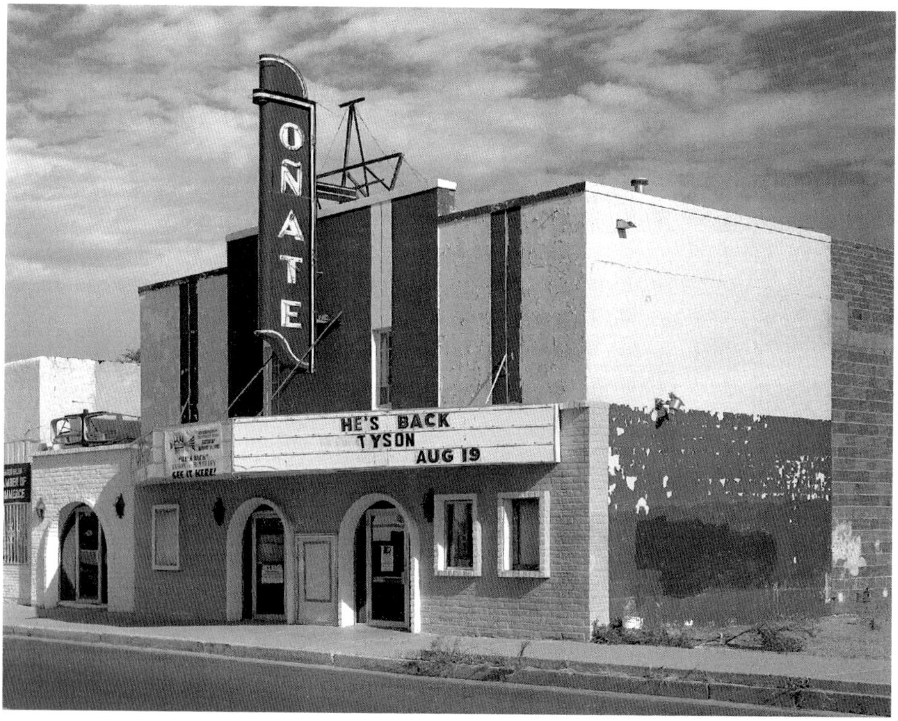

Oñate Theater, Belen. *Bob Christensen.*

The Founder, 2017's *The Space Between Us* and 2013's Ah-nold Schwarzenegger action comedy *The Last Stand*.

It is also notable for being the spot where the 1971 release *Bunny O'Hare* (which was nearly titled *Bunny and Claude*) spent a lot of time filming. This low-budget comedy starred Bette Davis and Ernest Borgnine as elderly bank robbers masquerading in hippie garb. In one scene, the Oñate Theater stands, with the marquee offering *The Case of the Missing Bank Robber* as that day's feature. Davis later sued, saying she was lied to about the script, but the lawsuit was dropped. The Oñate, sadly, is closed. Until recent times, it had become a restaurant, filled with nostalgia, including items from the theatre itself.

The Oñate Theater opened in 1932 with a seating capacity for six hundred patrons. It was named for an original Spanish colonizer of New Mexico who is often seen, rightfully, as a villain, but the Oñate closed in the early 1990s and was purchased in 1993 by local businessman Anthony Baca, who transformed it into a popular restaurant called Harla Mays. But it, too, is out of business. The building is vacant at this writing.

Two other theatre names pop up for Belen, the Central and the Cortez, both operating in the 1950s, with the Cortez offering 450 spaces for derrieres. But there is no concrete evidence of this readily available.

POINTING 'EM NORTH

Heading back northeast now, our next visit will be to Roy, a small ranching community on the high plains. Although three theatres are listed in various places that supposedly once operated in the village, only one can be proven: the Mesa. Other names cited include the Pendick in 1935 and the Real, which is said to have operated from 1940 to 1945.

But the Mesa was real. It probably was opened during World War II and perhaps shut down in 1950; it is long since abandoned but was once owned by Jerry and Annie Dikeman. Oddly, when I tried to call the Village of Roy for information, there was no phone number, and the chamber of commerce didn't answer the phone or have voicemail.

Wagon Mound, named for a nearby butte that kind of looks like a covered wagon, is briefly noted for having the 130-seat Wagon Mound Theater, open during the 1940s. But Springer, just a popcorn throw from Wagon Mound, did have a theatre, one that lasted almost eighty years. The Pastime was open as early as 1917, as witnessed by a notation in the ancient theatre trade publication *Artcraft Advance*. In a column by Julian Solomon Jr., he mentioned that "from away out in Springer, N.M., the Pastime Theatre sends us a letter…your Artcraft Advance is read from cover to cover, and we obtain many good points from its columns."

The Pastime stumbled into hard times, closing in 1937, but it reappeared with a new owner, Gibraltar Enterprises, with Zia being the new name. The Zia showed films from 1937 until October 1995 to as many as 350 happy patrons before financial issues caught up to it. It is still standing and is very photogenic; it once employed the late Charlene Baldwin as an usherette for fourteen years. You learn a lot from small-town obituaries.

Heading a bit farther north to Maxwell, there was rumor of the Maxwell Theater operating in this tiny town from 1940 to 1945, but nothing factual was found to verify this.

The town of Clayton is in far northeast New Mexico, where the Luna Theater is still in operation, but it deserves space in this book since it is also in the National Register of Historic Places. Opened in February 1917 as the Mission Theatre, the name change to the Luna probably happened in the 1930s, allowing the theatre to have the coolest marquee in all of New Mexico: a winking moon. It had the same owners for many years, the Herztein family, who sold it to Toller and Baca, who then peddled it to the ever-growing Gibraltar Enterprises in 1935. The sale of the theatre brought on much-needed refurbishing, and the grand reopening feature starred Shirley Temple in *The Little Colonel*. Many people were turned away from sold-out shows, and a competition was held that allowed girls to write essays about the Luna, with winners receiving free passes.

The Mission Theater encouraged residents of Clayton to experience "blazing the trail of love and civilization" during its showing of *The Iron Horse*, which was released in 1924. In the basement of the theatre, there was once a ballroom with a beautiful wooden floor that later became a roller skating rink. In the 1990s, a water pipe broke during some street construction, ruining the old floor. But this also helped kick-start the restoration of the four-hundred-seat auditorium.

In 1984, it was sold to Nancy Leighton and Roy Dean. Dean had been working as a projectionist to help pay the bills, and the duo's dedication kept the Luna up and running until 2006. It was later purchased by the Town of Clayton, and with financial help from a New Mexico MainStreet capital outlay grant and volunteers who stepped forward, the ancient building was revitalized, fixing a bad roof and lousy heating. The moon still winks every weekend at the Luna.

The Trail Drive-In once had space for 250 cars. The Trail was also owned at one time by Gibraltar after being sold by Murphy Theatres, headquartered in nearby Raton, New Mexico. Certainly open in 1960, historical records show that it operated from 1955 to 1985.

In nearby Des Moines, the Liberty Theater operated during the mid-1920s, according to a long-gone, oddly named local newspaper, the *Swastika*, which has nothing to do with what you might think. The paper was absorbed by the *Grenville News* and only published from 1913 to 1925. There is no other information about the Liberty readily available.

The once booming coal mining town of Dawson is now and has long been a ghost town. However, when it boomed, it *really* boomed, according to Kathy Weiser via the Legends of America website (legendsofamerica.com):

> *In 1910, the Dawson Opera House was the largest theatre in New Mexico. The Manager of the Opera House was George W. Murdock, followed by T.L. Kinney, a lawyer and later, a Judge. The seating in the Opera House was listed as 800 Orchestra seats, 200 Balcony seats including 30 boxes which held 6 people. The average prices were: Orchestra, $1.50 ($1.50 in 1920 = $35.10 in 2010); Balcony, $1.00 ($23.40 in 2010); Plus, Admission, 50 cents for Children ($11.70 in 2010), and 75 cents for Adults ($17.55 in 2010). The prices were the highest in the state of New Mexico.*
>
> *The Opera House, was home for the theatre, a billiard hall, bowling alley, a ballroom, banquet rooms, lodge meeting rooms, and offices for the Welfare Department of the Phelps Dodge Corporation, which directed the social welfare of the entire town. The lodge and banquet rooms were on the upper floors. In January of 1926, it played "Where Was I?," a silent comedy that was released in 1925.*

Prior to that, in 1923, 478 movies were shown at the Dawson Opera House. However, Dawson, located in far north-central New Mexico, near the town of Cimarron, was a place laced with tragedy. At one time, the town boasted a population of nine thousand. As with most mining towns, it seemed to endure tragedy or a boom-and-bust cycle. Dawson experienced the former, suffering two huge mine explosions, one in 1913 and a second in 1923, killing nearly four hundred miners. Very little remains of the town, and the opera house is long gone as well.

A bit farther north is Raton, which is one of only two places where John Wayne made a movie in New Mexico. Chances are he was not in Raton to film *Without Reservations*, a 1946 romantic comedy, where second-unit crews were sent to work. But Raton and its residents have worked hard to keep independent cinema alive and well in their community. The 85 Drive-In went into business in 1950 with a car capacity listed at 350; it closed in 2004. Once again, the big movie moguls were present, as it was operated by Gibraltar until 1961 and Theatre Enterprises thereafter.

The Shuler, perhaps once called the Rex before 1920, opened in 1925 and generally was a house for live theatre. In those early days, it was named

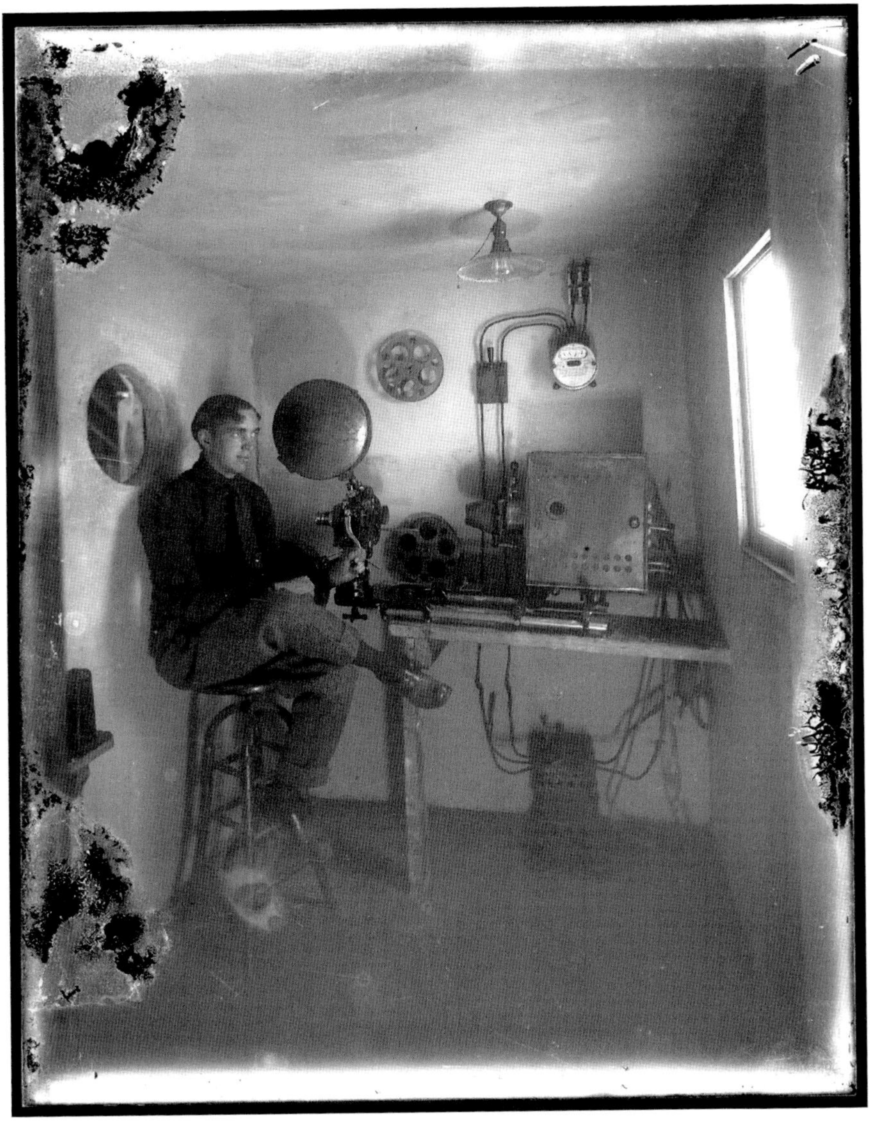

Projectionist, Raton, date unknown. *New Mexico State Archives, Palace of the Governors, Santa Fe, Raton Museum.*

the Shuler Auditorium after an early mayor of Raton who worked to get the project going. It offered opera, legitimate theatre, concerts and other forms of live entertainment. It wasn't until much later that the theatre offered movies, but by the 1950s, it had shut down. In the early 1960s, a theatre group began to use it, and since then, it has been used for live performance while undergoing renovation that started in the 1970s. It also boasts several WPA-era murals on the inside.

The El Raton remains the town's only true movie house, and even though it remains open, showing feature films on the weekends, it deserves to be mentioned here. It had its grand opening in April 1930; it's a very stylish movie palace with seating for 520. The theatre has a Spanish castle motif, which is reproduced throughout the interior of the building. The auditorium's screen resembles the theatre's façade of an ancient castle. With the sidewalls painted with floral designs, depicting vines growing over a Spanish style, it was designed to make the audience feel like they were sitting in a courtyard.

The theatre closed in 2006 but was purchased in 2008 by three local couples, who got it back on its feet once again. Of course, previous owners included Gibraltar and Theatre Enterprises.

In 2006, Dr. David Kammer submitted a multiple property listing titled "Movie Theaters in New Mexico built from 1905 to 1960" to the National Park Service for a National Register of Historic Places consideration. Within, he offered detail about booking films, which has been an issue for theatre owners and managers not connected with chains for years: "As was the case elsewhere, these independent theaters had a smaller seating capacity and were often located in the smaller towns. As a result, they often were forced to wait for popular films and, then, received older, often spliced copies of films. In order to overcome these limitations, several New Mexico theater owners joined other independent owners in Colorado, Nebraska and Utah to form Gibraltar Enterprises, a company that bought and booked films."

Consisting of a board of directors that included at least two mayors and theatre owners (who in some instances owned small local theatre chains), the company enabled its members to reduce booking and rental costs, thereby gaining leverage against the studio-owned theatre system. Included in this group in 1934 were the Silco, Lensic and El Raton Theatres. In 1935, T.F. Murphy also purchased the Mission Theater in Clayton, as the cooperative expanded to thirty-five theatres.

Although there are no known records for the company, it continued as a booking and film rental company until the mid-1950s, during the Great Depression and through the war decade. The efforts on the part of some independent theatre owners to band together to gain more leverage in acquiring and exhibiting films had an effect.

Kammer stated that only thirteen of the seventy-one theatres in the state affiliated with Hollywood's five major studios in 1940, with the

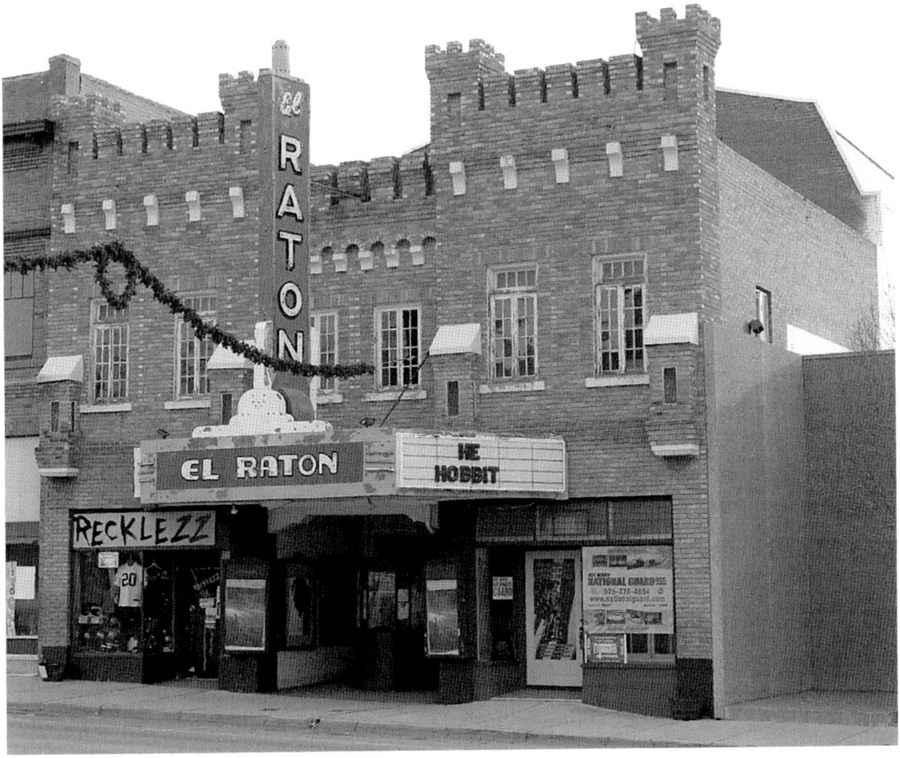

El Raton. *Wikimedia Commons.*

studios sending the big movies to their own theatres and excluding the independents. Numerous lawsuits came from this, and there was some justice seen over the years.

Raton also offered silent film lovers plenty of options during those days. Hugo Seaburg's Garden Coliseum offered silent flicks in 1908 before burning down in 1911. This amazing place could seat five thousand, which was nearly the entire populace of Raton at the time. There might have been as many as four other silent film emporiums, including one called the Lyric, during these days, along with several opera houses. Things certainly have changed.

Cimarron—it sounds so western, and it is. This pleasant little town, just down the road from Raton, is home to the historic St. James Hotel, which has seen author Will James, gunfights and maybe ghosts. It was also where the Cimarron Theater was located, with 237 seats. It sounds like it had the same ownership over the years, perhaps opening before World War II and closing sometime after 1972.

Farther down the road, just off I-25, is the city of Las Vegas, New Mexico, which has a remarkable film history. During the silent era, cowboy star Tom Mix came to town, tired of trying to find fresh locations to shoot films around Los Angeles. He shot several short films in and around Las Vegas, but all except *Local Color* have fallen victim to the ages.

Famed silent director Romaine Fielding also came to town and shot the first full-length feature film in and around Las Vegas. It was called *The Golden God*, but it was banned since it was "pro-labor" in a time when that was not considered a very good thing.

Las Vegas has a few up-and-running theatres, including the Indigo, the newest addition, and the cool and refreshing Fort Union Drive-In. But everything else is done for, including the Serf, Kiva, Duncan Opera House, Browne, Isis, Photoplay, Coronado, Plaza, Bijou and the Vegas Drive-In.

The Kiva opened in 1912 as the Mutual Theater. It was owned in 1939 by Frank Maloof, who remodeled the entire operation, giving it an Art Deco interior and plenty of neon outside. Maloof was way ahead of the times, having served as his own architect for the remodeling, which included a

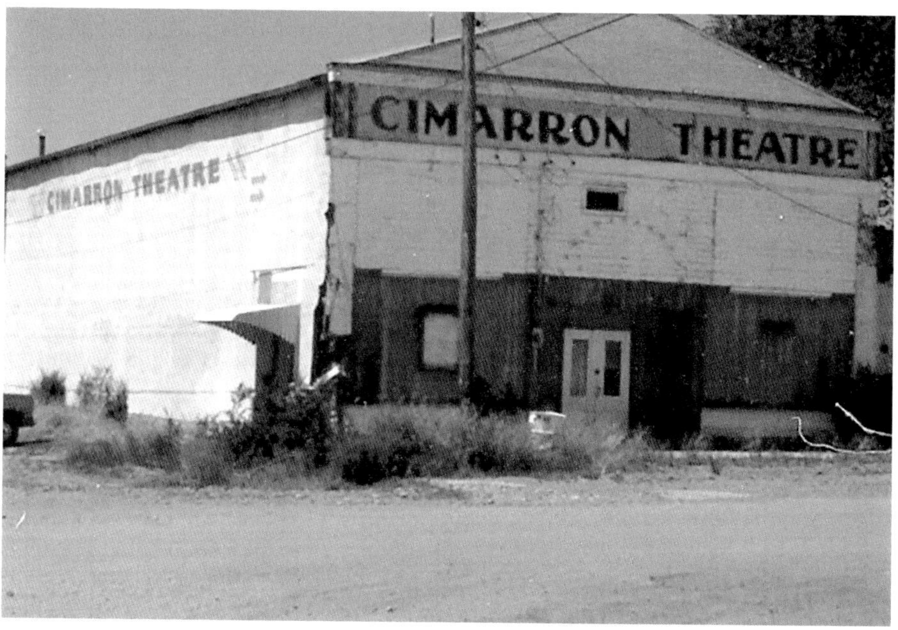

Cimarron Theatre, Cimarron. *From hopeseguin2010.wordpress.com.*

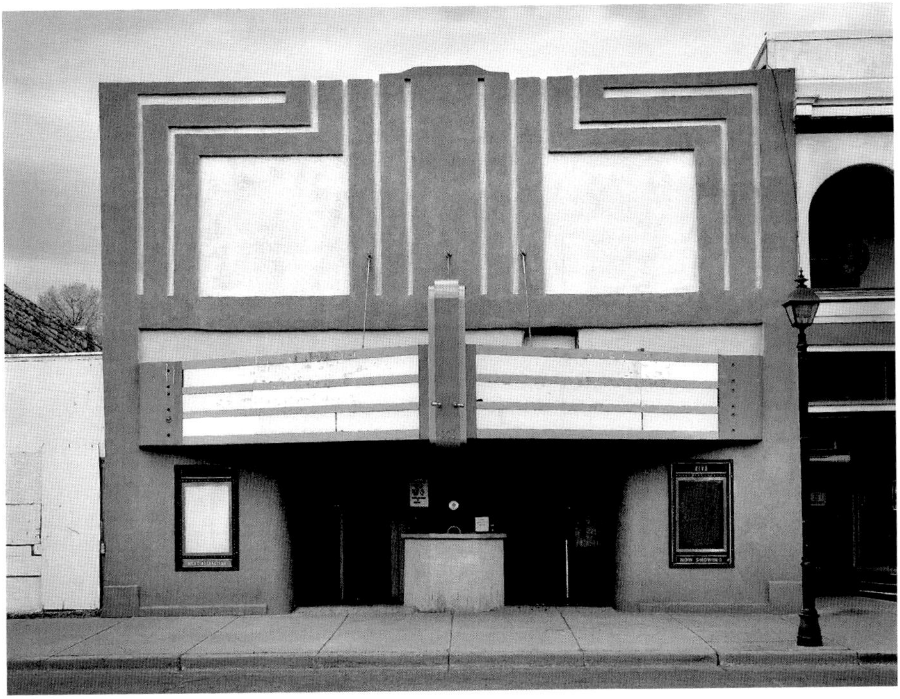

Kiva Theater, Las Vegas. *Bob Christensen.*

crying room for mothers (or fathers) with wailing children. It was mostly soundproof and allowed viewing through a plate glass window. It was also equipped with a speaker. Upon its original opening, it could hold four hundred or so patrons. Apparently, Maloof's enterprise was not totally successful. For a time, at least after World War II, it showed only Spanish-language features.

The Kiva was a Spanish-language house at the time and closed at some point, with Maloof still being the owner. Revived and renamed the Campus Theater in the 1960s, it became the Kiva Campus in the 1970s. The Kiva Campus closed again, date unknown, but was acquired by the Neal family, who reopened it in March 1991. By then, the seating capacity was 250. It seems that Maloof owned it for all those years, and upon his passing in the late 1990s, it was inherited by nephews of his by the name of Owens.

Sadly, the Kiva is the first theatre that I have researched for this book that closed because it was not able to afford to go digital. The building has been secured since 2013. The Serf, on the other hand, has enjoyed a great revival, although not as a movie house. Probably owned by the Maloof family, but possibly operated by Fox Intermountain, the Serf offered about seven hundred seats. The name came in an unusual way, via the initials of the four Maloof children: Sara, Eddie, Richard and Fannie. It was closed for many years before being purchased by the Romero and Moore families, who remodeled the old place into a music hall that is also available for weddings and meetings.

The Coronado, another enormous venue, opened in the fall of 1916, according to *Moving Picture Magazine*. It had more than seven hundred seats and three different owners, with it ostensibly closing in 1950. The article promised that the "air washer" would keep temperatures twenty degrees cooler than the outside. It was built for the Las Vegas Amusement Company.

The Browne (or Brown) was open during the silent era, possibly operated by the firm of Browne and Rosenwald, which also operated three other theatres in Las Vegas. To the delight of local audiences, it hosted a night of Tom Mix films, with the star himself in attendance; he asked them to treat him as "an ordinary citizen."

The Photoplay also was open during the silent era and played *The Closing Net* just after Christmas 1915, but the theatre may have been open as early as 1913. By 1926, it was gone.

The Duncan Opera House was primarily used for live entertainment but did show some cinematic epics in the 1930s, when it was owned by Fox Midwest Theaters.

No other information is on hand for the other theatres except the Vegas Drive-In, which is listed as being in business in 1960, maybe from 1955 to 1961, and capable of accommodating 350 cars. Oh and there's the Fort Union Drive-In—currently open seasonally. It was saved by public fundraising a few years ago that helped it go digital. Reports vary, but it seems likely that the Fort Union was opened in Ward around 1950 by Elaine Olson and H.C. Mitchell, who later sold it to Dollison Theaters. The Las Vegas, New Mexico website says 1958, however. It is now owned by Gilbert Pino. A story in the June 14 *Santa Fe New Mexican* quoted Jeanna Diluccio, who was the manager of the Fort Union for almost twenty years and who once called the drive-in "a place of the past, of a simpler time, a sweeter, gentler time." She "credits property owner Gilbert Pino with supporting it all these years. She said he could have easily torn it down and sold the land for top dollar."

There used to be a wonderful film festival in New Mexico—two, in fact. The best one was the Taos Talking Picture Festival, which ran from 1995 to 2003 before going bankrupt. Several small festivals have tried unsuccessfully to replace it, although the Taos Shortz had a fruitful run for ten years, pausing after its 2017 showcase. Taos as a town remains a blend of cowboys, artists, getting-away-from-its and those who desire to be some combination of all three.

Over the years, Taos has only had a few theatres come and go, such as the Kit Carson Drive-In, which allowed for two hundred cars and trucks and operated from the mid-1960s until closing for good, possibly in 1998. It was demolished, and now a Walmart (yuck!) stands on the spot where lots of heavy petting once took place. The Taos Theatre was located on the town plaza, operating from the 1930s until about 1960, offering seats to 450 happy patrons.

Several other screens might have been around as well, including the High Society, which opened in 1978 and was still operating via the Trans-Lux (Through Light) chain in 1992. But it, too, is deceased.

In nearby Rancho de Taos, the El Cortez was once owned and remodeled into a home and studio by actor and director Dennis Hopper, who lived in Taos for many years and is buried there. It offered seating for about three hundred, and as I write this, it is for sale for about $500,000. It has not been used as a movie palace for many years.

Now housing a spinning mill, the Liberty Theatre in the small town of Mora, according to a posting by Ken Roe on Cinema Treasures, was opened in the 1930s and lasted until the early 1970s. "There are plans to rehabilitate the theatre as a cinema and possibly performing arts venue." I don't think that will happen, as the economy in New Mexico can be bleak, which is sad to say, especially for arts organizations. No one answered the phone in three different places that I called to find out more information, so we will hope that it will be a theatre again someday.

Farther west from Taos is Chama, renowned for its fishing prospects and for the Cumbres and Toltec Railroad, a small rail line that hosts tourists and has been used in many movies, including *Butch Cassidy and the Sundance Kid*, *The Good Guys and the Bad Guys* and *Indiana Jones and the Last Crusade*. It was also the home of the Rainbow Theatre, which in its second life became a hardware store and is now a mini-mall, hosting several small local businesses. Word is that the Rainbow was only open for a few years during the 1950s and had room for two hundred guests.

There was also the Chama Drive-In, but other than a few photos of the screen on drive-ins.com, there are no details about the business.

Tierra Amarilla (yellow earth/soil in Spanish) is possibly the only unincorporated county seat in the state. The town has a very interesting history, which includes the Valley Theatre, long out of business but having had a brisk trade in the mid-1950s and 1960s, when it thrived. A National Park Service Register of Historic Places informational entry notes that it had "horse-shoe arranged wooden auditorium seats [ouch!], a 20-foot-wide stage and balcony with a projection booth. The building was built in 1935."

As an aside, in 1967, Reies Tijerina "raided" the Rio Arriba County Courthouse in Tierra Amarilla and attempted to make a citizen's arrest of the district attorney. His hope was "to bring attention to the unscrupulous means by which government and Anglo settlers had usurped Hispanic land grant properties." There was an armed struggle at the courthouse, with Tijerina and his supporters taking two hostages and heading south. Two men were injured, one being shot, and Tijerina was pursued by the Federal Bureau of Investigation (FBI), New Mexico National Guard and New Mexico State Police. After a lengthy trial, he served two years in a state penitentiary.

One of the oldest communities in the state is Espanola. About an hour north of Santa Fe, Espanola hasn't had too much movie house history over the years, although it was the home of the El Rio, which research finds was open in the 1940s, perhaps earlier, and was still in business in the late 1960s. It is long abandoned, but prior to its demise, it could host 650 supporters.

In 2008, an effort was made by the New Mexico House of Representatives—a lively if dysfunctional bunch if there ever was one—to spend $1.1 million to "plan, design, construct, renovate, and purchase" the old building. It never happened.

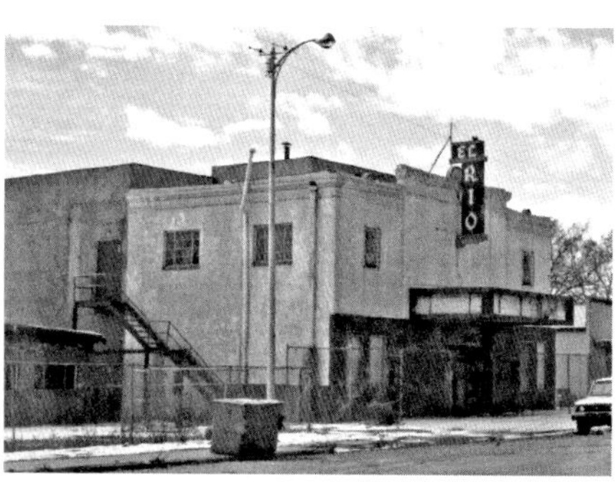

El Rio Theater, 1986, Espanola. *From cinematreasures.com, Don Lewis.*

The only other non-operating movie houses revealed in my research for Espanola are two drive-ins. The El Chico, opening in April 1959, had a name change to the Starlighter in 1962 and closed in 1994. It parked three hundred vehicles and only charged eight dollars per carload. Cheap! There was also the Rio Grande Twin, which was once operated by the small New Mexico–based chain Trans-Lux. This site closed in September 1999 after screenings of *The Blair Witch Project* and *The Sixth Sense*.

And the El Capitan, El Cine and El Villagra? Who knows! Names without faces. The banner year for the Villagra might have been 1935.

Up the road and hill from Espanola is the mysterious city of Los Alamos, birthplace of the atomic bomb and many things nuclear. A secretive place for many years, it remains that way now, but even pointy-headed scientists need to be entertained, hence a few movie houses have come and gone in Los Alamos and nearby White Rock. The first was named the Hill Theatre, which was established by the Atomic Energy Commission, which of course is all over Los Alamos. It opened on November 9, 1951, in the center of Los Alamos. Unlike many things in Atomic City, it was a nicely structured and modern building that also had room for stores upstairs and next door.

Our good friends at Theatre Enterprises ran the 994-seat theatre, with the first feature shown being *Angels in the Outfield*, starring Janet Leigh and Paul Douglas. It lasted less than four years, closing in 1955 and being remodeled into a department store, which it still houses.

According to the *Santa Fe New Mexican*, there was another Hill Theatre in Los Alamos. "The government built it as a wartime theater in 1943 and called it Theater Number One. It was renamed the Hill Theatre after the war and closed on July 1, 1950 and was purchased as surplus by a church and moved."

The Centre Theatre, with room for more than nine hundred, opened in 1948, screening *Sitting Pretty* with Clifton Webb.

The website for Conrad Skinner, a Santa Fe architect, offers a bit of history on the High Society Cinema in Los Alamos. Mr. Skinner redesigned the theatre, which looks very much like Santa Fe's Jean Cocteau Theater: "The High Society was a cinema in the first mall built in post–WWII Los Alamos, New Mexico. Trans-Lux bought the theater in the late 1980s and divided the original house into a triplex with a new lobby, new seating, acoustical treatments, projection optics and surround sound. In the lobby design, the curved ticket counter rotates the customer's attention to the vestibule and a counter-curved concession stand. Red fluorescent tubes glow in the ceiling." A beautiful and innovative spot. Sadly, the High Society closed, probably in 2001.

In nearby White Rock, the White Roxy Theatre, seating 193, was opened in late December 1972 by Eileen and Roger Moore (not *that* Roger Moore). This was a new idea in the world of movie houses, as the theatre came via a franchise agreement with United General Theatres, which was competing against the terribly operated Jerry Lewis Cinema franchises, both of which competed for family-type audiences (not screening R-rated movies at first).

According to United General's sales offering, like the Lewis franchise, which appeared in newspapers across the country in 1972, "the theatres were fully automated and could be run by two people. $15,000 plus operating costs was the price of the turnkey operation, with 16mm projection."

In a *Los Angeles Times* story, it was said that two hundred cinemas were planned in California alone, but by March 1973, the corporation had filed for bankruptcy. In 1975, the principal operators were indicted by a federal grand jury on twenty-four counts of conspiracy and mail fraud. Some major movie stars—Debbie Reynolds, Glenn Ford and Agnes Moorhead—were involved with the original project, but none was ever involved in the charges.

In February 1975, the *Los Alamos Monitor* reported that the White Roxy Theatre had been purchased by Taffy Gibney and Mary Rush. They planned to replace the 16mm projector with a 35mm projector to increase the selection of films. Information on the White Roxy Theatre's closing date is unknown. The Jerry Lewis debacle ended in 1980 when bankruptcy hit. Amusingly, some franchises stayed open, and others switched to adults-only fare.

NORTH BY NORTHWEST

Farther north and west is the town of Aztec, which also reportedly had a UFO crash, later proven to be a hoax. But it did play host to the Mayan, which opened its doors in 1927. The owner was one J. Oscar Manning. It was bought by the Allens in 1941, rebuilt and renamed the Aztec. The closure of the theatre took place sometime later; it first became a meeting hall for veterans and is now home to Crash Music, which uses it as a live music venue.

Also in Aztec were the Rincon and Yucca Drive-Ins, both in business during the drive-in boom days from the late 1950s (there is an old news ad for the Rincon from 1959) until possibly 1975. The Rincon hosted 250 autos and the Yucca 350.

Heading farther north to the upper northwest corner of New Mexico, one will find the city of Farmington, a busy oil town with one of the state's best museums, the Farmington Museum. It is operated by the city. Movie theatre history here too? Yup! Farmington has seen its share of cinematic auditoriums and drive-ins come and go, including the Apache Drive-In, which operated for an amazing sixty years, from 1954 to 2014. It could accommodate three hundred cars and was one of nearly fifty drive-in movie theatres that once dotted the state. It had two screens.

Information at www.driveintheatre.com notes that the first drive-ins in the state opened in 1948—three during that year, in fact. The pinnacle was 1958, though, when an amazing forty-nine were operating, but from there it declined. By 1987, there were only six, and now only two remain: the previously mentioned Fort Union in Las Vegas and the three-screen setting in Carlsbad, the Fiesta. Some beautiful outdoor screens that showed people things beyond the imagination are now parking lots or Walmarts. The screen of the Valley Drive-In made way for "progress." I was unable to secure other facts about this business.

Farmington is also where Allen Theatres, New Mexico's largest and most successful chain of theatres, began. Frank Allen moved to Farmington in 1893. His first theatre operation was the Allen Opera House, which opened in 1912 with a ten-cent admission price. He used his youngest daughter, Mary, to "cue" or play the piano for the silent films.

The Allen Theatre opened in 1922 and replaced the opera house, which like many theatres around the state burned down. The movie house showed its first talking picture in 1930, but Frank passed away in 1932. It appears that his wife/widow, Augusta, assumed operations and saw to the first installation of an air conditioner in 1937. In 1947, the Allen got its first concession stand, but the site closed in the 1970s. It also had a crying room for mothers who wanted to see a movie while taking the little one along with, a concept that eludes me (babies in a theatre, not crying rooms). Augusta went to the big picture house in the sky in 1946, and Russell, the oldest son, and his wife, Helen, assume command along with some business partners.

In 1948, the Totah opened its doors, screening *The Paleface*, starring Bob Hope. It closed as a movie theatre in 1982. It was dormant for many years, and Allen sold it in 2004. It is now a live event venue.

Way back in '52, the Apache became the city's first drive-in, followed by the Valley in 1954. Russell died in 1961, and the Crawfords, the other partners, would leave the business the next year, allowing for Larry Allen to buy the theatres from Helen Allen, Russell's widow.

The Cameo Theater opened in 1971, being the first "fully automatic" theatre. It was still in operation in 2007 but is now closed. The Allen family also operated the Centennial Twin from the mid-1970s through 2007. From there, the Allens have really spread their wings and currently have about one hundred screens in New Mexico and far southern Colorado. (I might add that their popcorn is probably the blandest and most hull-filled that I have ever had.)

In nearby Shiprock, the Chief Drive-In entertained the masses prior to 1955 until 1980. It allowed for 250 automobiles. Due south from Shiprock, on a U.S. highway that used to be US 666, we arrive in Gallup, home of numerous silver screens.

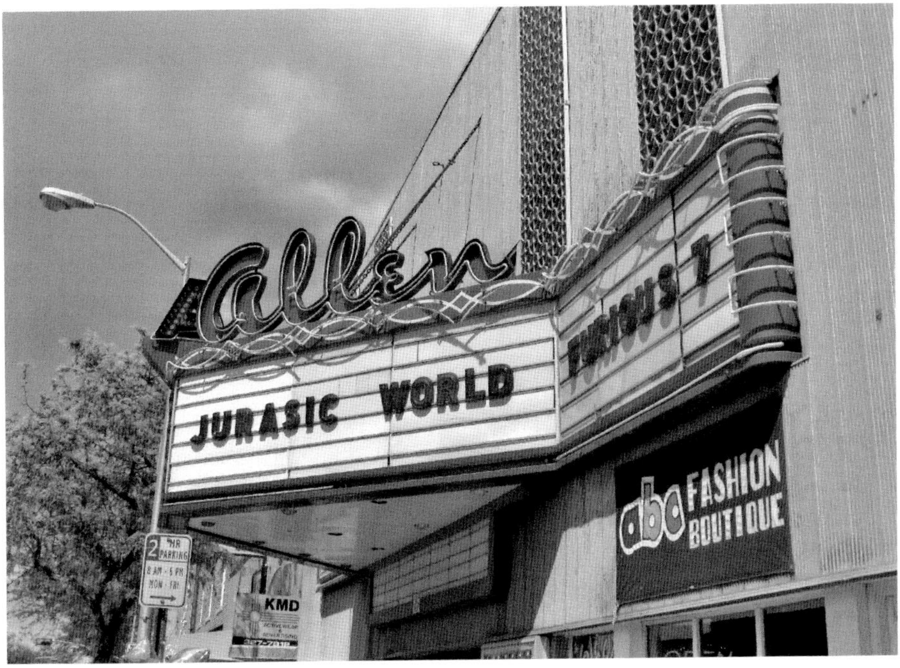

Allen Theatre, Farmington, New Mexico, 2015.

The first modern theatre was built here in 1920 and was originally called the Strand. It opened on March 2, 1920, screening a ten-reel program. Until 1928, when the still operating El Morro opened, the Strand is said to have been one of Gallup's main entertainment sources.

Before the Strand, several other cinemas could be found in Gallup, mostly nickelodeons. But the Strand changed all of that with its banked floor, a balcony and a large seating capacity. The local press offered up that one thousand people came out for the grand opening and that the Strand showed many of the major silent films of the times and, later, talking pictures.

In 1936, the Strand was under the ownership of R.E. Griffith, and the theatre was completely redone, inside and out, in what is called Pueblo Deco style. Griffith also changed the name to the Chief Theater. It is no longer a movie cinema, having become a retail store sometime after 1972. The building, which doesn't really resemble a theatre any longer, was added to the National Register of Historic Places on May 16, 1988, and the State of New Mexico Register of Historic Places in 2000. Its famed vertical sign and marquee, which dated back to the 1930s, was lost in the 1970s when hit by lightning.

The Rio West Twin opened in 1976. It was operated by Allen Theatres. This theatre closed in August 2003.

Gallup also landed two drive-ins. The Zuni, which had a single screen and nearly six hundred parking spaces, was owned at the end (probably 1985) by Commonwealth Theatres. There was also the Yucca Drive-In, which has scant facts, but it was open, like most of these theatres, in October 1956 and operated by Theater Enterprises. If I owned a theatre, I don't think I would call it the Yucca, since every single one that I have researched is out of business.

Other theatres that may have existed in Gallup at one time include several indoors: the Cairo, which newspaper ads indicate was open in 1934–35; the Navajo, possibly operated throughout the 1940s by Theater Enterprises; and the Rex, which opened in 1924 and was owned by noted opera composer Giacomo Puccini.

The Reel Theater may have operated during World War II, but no other information is available on this business.

Then there is the terrific and still operating El Morro. "The theatre's original owners were Elizabeth and William Nagel. The Nagel family built the El Morro Theatre in 1928 [opening in August of that year], considering

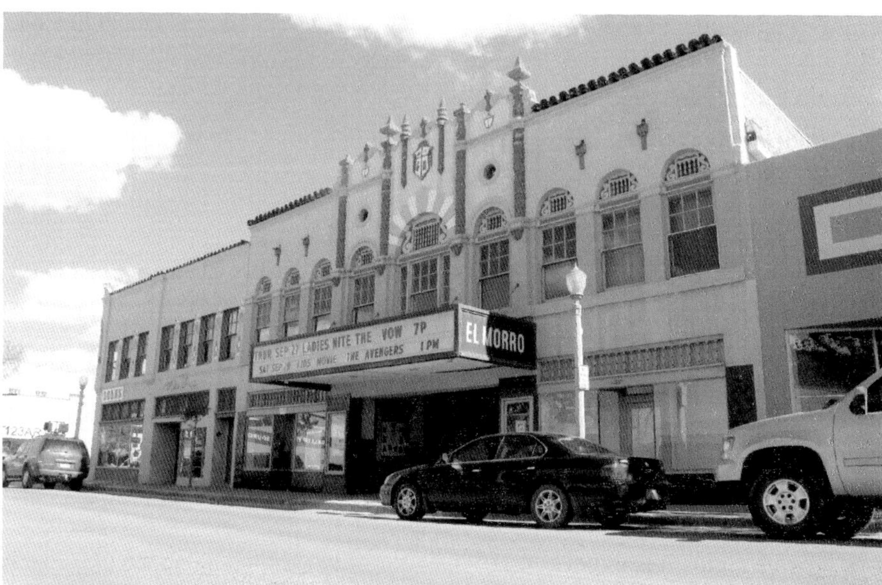

El Morro Theatre, Gallup. *By TheBackWoodsRevival (own work)* [CC BY-SA 3.0], *via Wikimedia Commons.*

the venue a serious concert theatre, modeled after the grand places in the east," said Jennifer Lazarz, who is the tourism and marketing manager for the City of Gallup. This is from an interview with Helen Radosevich, who turned ninety in August 2016 and was an usher at the El Morro from 1939 until the mid-1940s:

> *There was a cry room on both the main floor and balcony. The lobby featured a large Navajo woven rug, but no concessions. The Nagels didn't want any food or beverage in the theatre. The doors opened, you were seated, and a music program began at 6:30pm, 30 minutes before the silent film. The program included pipe organ (on a Reuter Pipe Organ still in existence today—it resides in the Reuter Organ Showroom in Lawrence, KS) played by Pearl Booth Masters. On the weekends the audience was treated to a live orchestra before and during the films: "Tony Diaz and His Orchestra."*
>
> *The theatre itself was marvelous—none of the brown "beams" (which are fake) were in the theatre. Instead the ceiling was covered in a painting similar to the sky, there were four murals on the walls, three chandeliers, and lush velveteen curtains. Behind those lush curtains were sheer flat curtains painted with a mural so that the image would glow in front of the screen and part to reveal the screen itself. The dressing rooms were under the stage adorned with long red curtains, clothing racks, and full length mirrors.*

The theatre is open today, only closing sporadically for updating and renovation. It went through the usual string of owners that have been involved in theatre operations through the ages and was purchased by the City of Gallup in 2003 from the Gallup Catholic School Foundation. It screens movies weekly and special events as well and is one of the state's coolest venues.

Down the road, heading east to Grants, which once was a hub for uranium mining in New Mexico, we find that this community also has a history of closed cinemas, including the Lux. A posting on Cinema Treasures proffers the following:

> *The owner of the West Theatre was J.C. West, Grants' theater magnate. He bought the Lux Theatre in 1950, and built the Sahara Drive-In in 1958. He also operated the Trails Drive-In at Grants. The September 18, 1937, issue of* Boxoffice *had this to say about the Lux Theatre: "Souris & Ade are opening the Lux at Grants, N.M., a house of 518 seats. The town has been without a theatre since 1930."*

> *Another item in the same issue lists various pieces of equipment and furnishings installed at the Lux by the Denver branch of National Theatre Supply Company. Neither item indicates whether the Lux was new construction or a renovation of an older theater—perhaps the one that had closed in 1930, which may have been called the Grants Theater.*
>
> *West, who would later build the West Theatre in Grants, bought the Lux from C.E. Means in 1950. He might have closed the Lux for a time in the 1960s. Then the January 30, 1967, issue of* Boxoffice *said that J.C. West had opened the Lux after an extensive remodeling. He intended to operate the house with an art film policy.*
>
> *West was still operating the Lux as late as February 1970, when the* Boxoffice Magazine *issue of the 16th said that the house had to be closed for one night due to a fire in a furnace blower.*

The West is still in business as a first-run twin-screen theatre in downtown Grants. It began showing flicks in 1959. It cost $125,000 to build, and the opening features were the immortal *Tarawa Beachhead* and *Crash Landing*, which starred Nancy Reagan.

The Sahara opened in 1958, east of town, operating until 1975, and was demolished sometime after that. It could accommodate four hundred vehicles, and its opening film was *Battle Cry*, with Van Heflin.

The Trail, located north of town, possibly closer to the small village of Milan, seemingly was in business from 1964 to 1975, hosting as many as three hundred cars. The *Cibola Beacon* newspaper observed that "the Trail Drive-in Theater officially opened in April. The first features shown were 'The Young Swingers,' with nine hand-clapping hootenanny hits, and 'Thunder Island,' about a hired gun in the Caribbean." Sorry I missed this double feature!

On a sad note for movie history, a plane crash on March 22, 1958, killed movie producer Mike Todd, the husband of actress Elizabeth Taylor, twenty-two miles southwest of Grants in rural Cibola County. The *Grants Beacon* reported:

> *City officials were swamped with calls after Todd was killed in a crash of his two-engine Lockheed Lodestar. The producer had become famous for his recent movie "Around the World in 80 Days." The location was two miles north of the Ice Caves. Todd had been in Albuquerque to promote that film.*
>
> *Telephone calls to the* Beacon, *the radio station, and the Grants police station came from New York, Hollywood, Calif., and London, England.*

Liz Taylor called the Grants Police Station to verify the report and broke into hysterical sobs when told the news, according to media accounts.

Apparently, Todd's private plane "iced up" and was heavily overloaded when it crashed during a thunderstorm in the mountains southwest of Grants. Also killed were screenwriter Art Cohn and two pilots, Bill Verner and Tom Barclay. Somewhat eerily, the plane was called the *Lucky Liz*.

Cuba is our next stop. Located northwest of Albuquerque, it was once the place where the Placitas Hills Drive-In was located, south of town. It was owned and operated by W. Edge and had a capacity of two hundred. There are no open or closed dates to the drive-in, but it was demolished.

Just down the road in Bernalillo, where we draw closer and closer to our final destinations of Albuquerque and Santa Fe, there was the Zia Theater. In case you are wondering, the Zia symbol is the official state symbol of New Mexico, hijacked from people of the Zia Pueblo. Now it appears most everywhere.

James and Ella Silva built and owned the 150-seat Zia Theater in 1938, operating it with their six kids. The original name was Tiguex. The *Albuquerque Journal* reported in 2005 that "master carpenter Clemente Salazar built it at a cost of $1,500. The screen, projector, popcorn machine, and the 1905 Moorish-style light fixtures came from the remodeled Lensic Theatre in Santa Fe, owned by Nathan Salmon."

The Zia Theater was closed in 1950 because a highway was changed from two to four lanes, knocking thirty feet off the building. Presently, the building is occupied by a business called the Pottery House, which is part of a row of buildings extending down from the theatre, most of which were once owned by the Silvas.

Although listed on a website or two, there are no concrete details about two other possible showbiz palaces: the Coronado (possibly closed by 1945) and the dully named Bernalillo (closed by 1940, maybe).

CITY OF DUKES

ALBUQUERQUE

At last we have arrived in New Mexico's largest city, which may have been named by early settlers who couldn't pronounce the Spanish word for apricot, *albaricoques*. Several theories exist, but that is my favorite.

To try to cover all the theatres that have come and gone in Albuquerque would take another entire book. So, in this section, I will touch on those with the most interest, such as the Circle Autoscope, the Guild and the old, old Orpheum, as well as try to touch on the others briefly. According to the CinemaTour website, there are forty-five out-of-business but definitive movie houses. Cinema Treasures only lists twenty-nine, and neither offers up the ages-old Orpheum.

The Don Pancho Art Theater was one of the city's and state's first "arthouse" theatres, concentrating on foreign, revival and independent films, along with film-related events. Its history is a bit murky, but newspaper ads offer information on screenings in 1962, and the *Caliche County Rendering Works*, an alternative paper of the times, carried a schedule for the theatre in 1968. Keif Henley shared that it closed in about 1990. "It was owned by Joseph Esposito, a lawyer from Tucson, who also owned The Loft." That theatre is thriving and is Tucson's art/indie venue deluxe.

Today, the only independent theatre in a city of 450,000 is the Guild, owned by my friend Keif Henley. "Peter Conheim was my business partner. I bought him out in 2009," Henley said. "I've co-owned and owned the

Guild Cinema since 2004 and bought it from Pangaea Cinema LLC, Janet Braziel and Sylvia Wittels."

The theatre, prior to Henley's ownership, was open as early as 1963, probably as an arthouse venue as well, as it first screened the Oscar-nominated Greek film *The Red Lanterns*. A post on one website opines that the theatre was for adult fare, which is not accurate. The Guild later became a revival house and had the same owner as the Don Pancho, but it closed in 1977, opening its doors again in 1979 as a true arthouse cinema. Briefly closed in 1998, it has been in business since, with Henley as the jack-of-all-trades—owner, booker, projectionist, concessionaire and ticket seller—since 2004.

Albuquerque and New Mexico's climate in general have always allowed for drive-ins to prosper. At various times, the Duke City sported at least ten and possibly more. The Tesuque Drive-In was one of the most successful, holding 650 cars, and was owned by Cliff Butler in 1966.

Certainly the most unique drive-in was the Circle Autoscope, which opened in June 1963. Not your usual outdoor cinema, the Circle had individual screens for each car, which would seem to me like you were watching television from your car. Each screen was sixty inches, "one for every car. The screens were arranged in a circle, the center of which contained the projection house." The projector was made up of a "fly's eye lens," which was a cluster of small lenses. The film was beamed through the lens and then reflected off mirrors, through portholes in the building and onto the individual screens by rear projection. Sound was of the conventional variety. The concept was unique but not appreciated, and all 260 screens were dark by 1965. A poster on Cinemea Treasures recalled this about the Sunset Drive-In, located in southwest Albuquerque:

> *The earliest I remember about the drive in was when I was probably six or seven years old, which is around 1976 or 1977. Back then it was owned by Commonwealth Theaters and it showed mainly Spanish movies. My dad worked for the company then, and we lived on the property. It was closed down sometime around 79 or 80, but was purchased by a private owner and they showed a mix of English and Spanish movies. They were 2nd run movies that had already been in theatres but people still came out to see them....I worked there for a couple of years in 83 and 84 before it finally shut down for good.*

The sun eventually set on the Sunset.

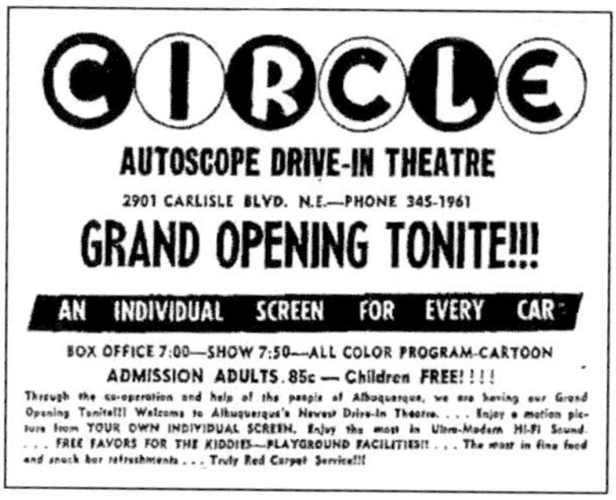

Left: Newspaper ad for Circle Autoscope Drive-In, Albuquerque. *From drive-ins.com.*

Below: Sunset Drive-In marquee, Albuquerque. *Randy Carlisle.*

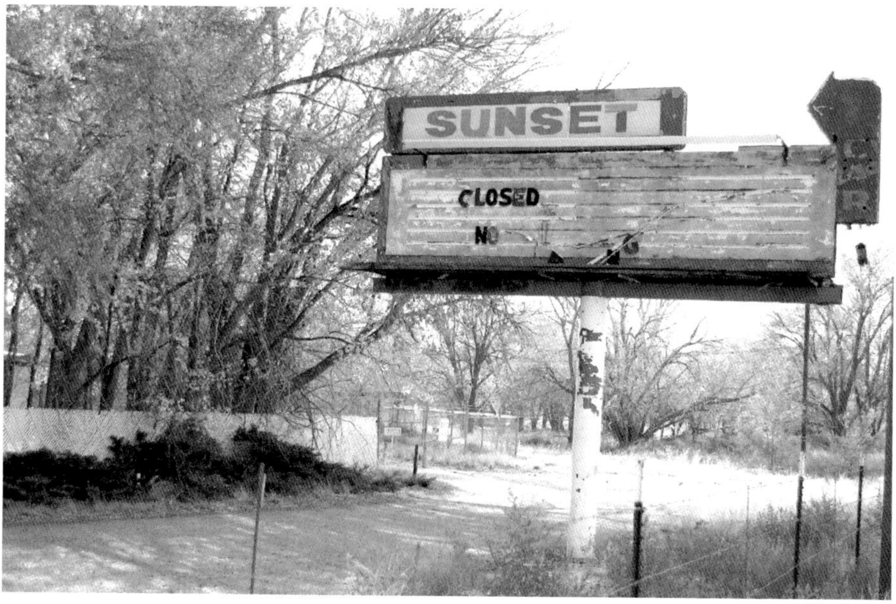

The Ernie Pyle Theater was named after the great Pulitzer Prize–winning journalist, who called Albuquerque home for many years before his death in 1945. In about 1950, the theatre opened with 650 seats, but it only lasted until 1955. It was later demolished for a freeway extension.

In reviewing the list of theatres that once were up and running in Albuquerque, I note, for the first time, that there were a lot of adult theatres through the years, including the Backdoor, Madam X, The Hut and the Master, among others. We'll spare you the details, but the 1970s were hot times for such venues. There was also a drive-in, along Interstate 25 in the heart of the city, that had multiple screens, and at the end of its life, it was playing adult fare, with expected results on the freeway. It is said that in 1971, 720 of the 14,450 operating movie theatres in the United States were showing adult entertainment.

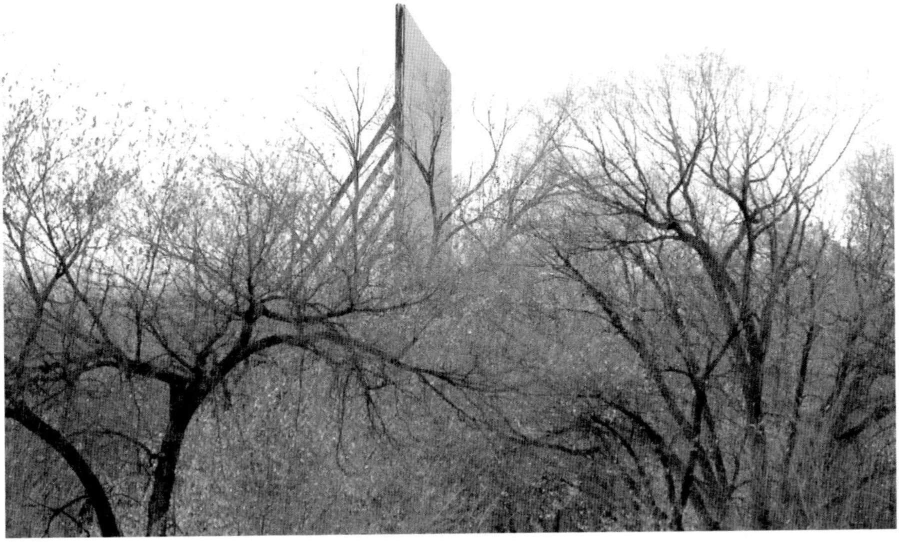

How many people were entertained by moving images on the now abandoned screen of Albuquerque's Sunset Drive-In? *Randy Carlisle.*

A more recent loss was the Cinema East, which entertained the masses from 1964 to 1985. It started as a single screen and then was "twinned" in 1972 before shuttering in 1985, when operated by Commonwealth Theatres.

Other historical cinemas include the Orpheum, Lobo, Kimo, El Ray, Hiland and Sunshine. The Orpheum, which apparently opened in 1911, was built on the site of a furniture store (which had burned down) by the same owner of the store. It offered vaudeville and had its own stock company and other live performances—one by the "amazing and wonderful Arzalia who could answer any question" and who drew two thousand people to his/her show in December of that year. According to Mo Palmer's *Stories of Albuquerque* blog, another one thousand were turned away. Palmer goes on to relate that in 1911,

> Albuquerque Morning Journal *treated all of Albuquerque's children to a 3 o'clock matinee at the Orpheum—provided they came by the office for a ticket first. Ads reassured nervous moms: The theatre had 11 exits and stationed extra ushers at each egress; the theatre was concrete, not the cheap veneer of fricasseed Futrelle's* [the crispified furniture store, Futrelle being the owner]. *The children were shown vaudeville, 10 girls who would "dance and sing for the edification of the children" and*

> *two reels of "Dante's Inferno." Reviews note its frightening images and classify it as a horror film.*

By 1919, the Orpheum had become a dance hall. Amazingly, it apparently did not burn again and is now still in use in 2017 as an arts space.

Competition for the Orpheum during those early days of flickers came from several sources; the Elks, the Gem, the Pastime (or PassTIme as it is sometimes spelled) and the Crystal. The Crystal was another enormous enterprise, seating more than 1,100. It opened in October 1911 but was out of business by 1931.

The other locations have little available history, but it seems that all had live performances, such as vaudeville and silent films during their glory days. Another place lost to time is an eight-hundred-seater, originally known as the Isleta. It opened on December 23, 1948, operated by Marshall Brothers. Later, All States Theatres modernized and renamed it the Esquire Theatre in 1958. It was later acquired by Flach and Pierce of El Paso. In 1959, it was acquired by Rudy Napoleone and became a Spanish-language theatre, hosting live performances by Mexican film stars. The Isleta/Esquire closed in 1962 and became a grocery store. The building was later demolished and is now a park.

The Lobo, now a church, opened in 1939 and lasted on and off until mid-2000. The Lobo was considered a "suburban" theatre at the time, as it was the first movie house built away from downtown Albuquerque. It had either five hundred or seven hundred seats, depending on which source you believe, and was also managed on and off by Blanche Hatton, who started her theatre management career in Albuquerque in 1924. There is some information posted on Cinema Treasures that offers this neat little story about her prowess:

> *Miss Hatton was closing the Lobo late one night (she was alone in the theatre) when, with the "petty cash box" in hand, she was met with an armed intruder in the Lobo lobby.*
>
> *"Give me the cash!" the robber demanded.*
>
> *"You want the cash?" Miss Hatton asked. "Here," she said, "take it!"*
>
> *Miss Hatton hurled the cash box at the intruder. The weight of the contents of the box was sufficient to knock the pathetic, hapless robber unconscious. When the cops arrived, the bad guy was arrested, and Miss Hatton deposited the receipts early the next morning. By the way, she was close to eighty years old when she took out the punk, who was 60 years her junior.*

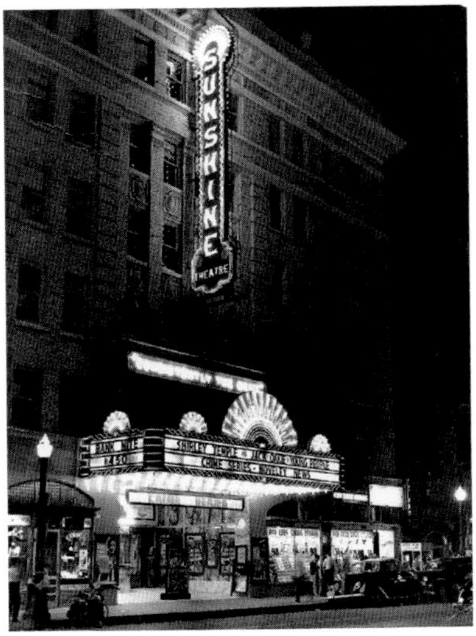

Sunshine Theatre, 1940, Albuquerque. *Albuquerque Film Office.*

The Kimo opened in 1927 and over the years has come and gone, but the site is now a major player for live events and special film screenings. The word *kimo* is loosely translated from the Tewa Pueblo language, meaning "king of its kind." It is a beautiful venue, said to be haunted by the ghost of six-year-old Bobby Darnall, who died there in 1951 after a boiler explosion.

The Hiland opened with stadium seating and more than 1,100 seats in 1950, lasting until 1995. It has been closed on and off since then and was once used as a music venue. It now hosts a dance school.

The Sunshine started showing movies in 1924 and was the city's first big movie house, with 1,100 seats. By the 1980s, it had closed and is now used as an all-ages nightclub.

Giacomo Puccini, the great opera composer, also had a hand in the El Rey, which swung its doors open on June 27, 1941, lasting as such until mid-1969, when it became the Reel Art Theatre, a tricky moniker for a movie house that started playing adult movies such as *The Lustful Turk* and *Bachelor's Dream*. It closed in '72 and was originally owned by Claude Graves.

The Albuquerque Drive-In operated from 1978 to 1995 and was torn down in 1996 and replaced by a twenty-four-screen indoor theatre. This might have been the drive-in that showed the adult films that caused havoc on the freeway. Rumor has it that the 66 Drive-In showed adult fare after the regular features.

THE CITY WEIRD

SANTA FE

Our last stop on this statewide tour is Santa Fe, which at one time was said to have more moviegoers per capita than any other city in the country except for New York. That is probably no longer true, now that too damn many people sit at home and watch movies online or on DVD, and we have lost seven screens recently to boot.

I am guilty of that myself, but if there is a movie I do want to see while it is in a theatre, I make every effort to see it on a *real* screen with other people who are there for some of the same reasons I am. And I only watch films online if they are not available in any other format.

How many of you can remember the first time you watched a video or DVD or something online and what the circumstances were? I do remember my first VHS viewing, watching *Jeremiah Johnson*, which I had seen in a theatre long before the VHS came out, with my leman of the time, Nancy, and her co-worker Jeannette, who had rented a VCR and a few movies.

My first real date was in the Chicago Theater with my girl friend Joan, who I had a huge crush on, even though she ignored me unless I bought her something or took her somewhere. Well, took her I did, on the train from our hometown to downtown to the Chicago to see—it's *so* embarrassing now—*Valley of the Dolls*. The Chicago had about 3,500 seats, and there were maybe 100 people in the whole place. We sat in the balcony.

My hoped-for session of necking and light petting never came to be for two reasons. Joan said no. And some creep came upstairs to the balcony, which had rows of empty seats, and immediately sat down next to Joan and put his hand on her leg. Joan didn't take kindly to this. She swatted him as hard as she could with her large, impervious handbag and yelled, "Take your hand off me, you firetrucker" (paraphrasing). The slob made a hasty retreat, and I kept my hands to myself.

I digress. Santa Fe has had many theatres over the years, including many arthouses. Today, it can proudly say that it only has two set of screens via a chain; everything else is independent. In the silent era, places such as the Santa Fe Opera House and the Elks Opera House added films to their menu, and by 1907, the *Santa Fe New Mexican* was reporting that "moving pictures are becoming very popular…with crowds increasing nightly." A few years after opening, the Elks brought in professional management—Keefe, Kaune and Koch—and the theatre was renamed the Kays.

Nathan Salmon became a big name in the Santa Fe movie business, opening the now restored and operating Lensic Theater and, prior to that, the Paris Theater, a 1,056-seat affair that became the city's first real cinema. It opened on August 15, 1914, with *The Wrath of the Gods.* One can find the history of the amazing Lensic from a website dedicated to the site (Lensic.org):

> *Down to his last coins and stuck in Santa Fe by a snowstorm, Nathan Salmon pawned his watch to a friend and resumed his career as a cart peddler.*
>
> *Success did not elude him and he soon became a successful and respected businessperson.*
>
> *"I made all my money here and I wanted to give the people something to show my appreciation,"* [said] *Nathan Salmon on building the Lensic Theater.*
>
> *Salmon, originally from Syria, along with his son-in-law, E. John Greer, announced on March 27, 1930, plans for a "Spanish-style" theatre which would contain the latest projection and sound equipment—and would offer live performances and "talkies" to Santa Fe's 11,000 residents.*
>
> *The project moved swiftly. Architects convened in April, blueprints were ready by July, and ground was broken on September 26, 1930. That same day, Salmon offered a \$25 prize for an appropriate name for the new theatre—preferably Spanish, or one incorporating the initials of his grandchildren. The winning combination came from Mrs. P.J. Smithwick, whose acronym "Lensic" not only combined the desired initials (for the children, Lila, Elias John, Nathan, Sara, Mary Irene, and Charles), but also suggested the "lens" of a movie projector and the scenic splendor of the theater's interior.*

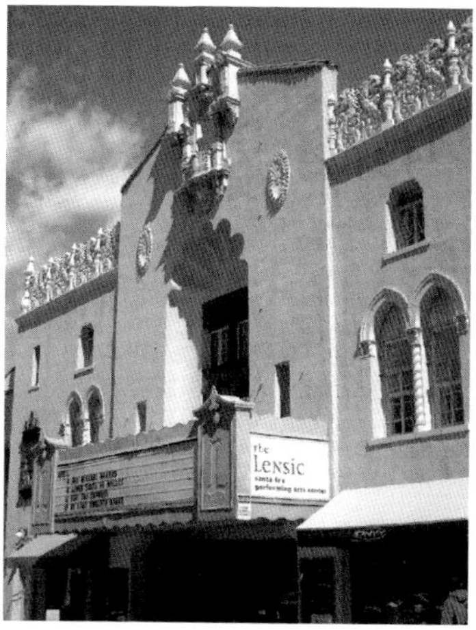

Lensic Theater, façade, Santa Fe. *Photo by Ysabel Velarde.*

During the 1950s, the Lensic thrived. However, as the city grew, other entertainment options became available. It went through the usual owners—Frontier, Gibraltar, Commonwealth and United Artists. The technical requirements of modern performance continued to surpass those offered by the old Lensic. In the 1990s, while managed by United Artists, the theatre stopped hosting live events and, in 1999, closed its doors altogether.

Bill and Nancy Zeckendorf, members of a distinguished real estate family in New York, moved to Santa Fe in the 1980s and were among the first to understand the potential of the Lensic as a performing arts center. Determined to provide the city with such a venue, they returned to Salmon's vision of a dramatic showplace.

Working with eight Santa Fe performing arts groups, the city government, individuals and business leaders, they raised $9 million from the community, recruited a respected board of directors and incorporated the theater as a nonprofit.

The location reopened in 2001. Over the years, the theatre has hosted many people of repute, including Errol Flynn, Judy Garland, Ronald Reagan, Roy Rogers and the late great character actor Ben Johnson. Salmon's success encouraged him to purchase the Kays, which received a name change to the Rialto, operating as same until 1926, when a live theatre group took over the venue. By 1939, the building had been torn down.

Salmon hired a famed theatre architect by the name of Carl Boller, from Los Angeles, to remodel the Paris, offering him "a Navajo blanket for all the seats you can give me over the thousand mark." The new palace opened again on January 6, 1929, and two years later played Santa Fe's first sound film. Sadly, the Paris burned in 1945, but in its stead the El Paseo opened.

Late 1948 brought another theatre into the fold, one day before the opening of the slightly smaller El Paseo. The Santa Fe Theater opened with seating for 877, 200 more than the El Paseo, and it opened big with a screening of a Michael Redgrave film from England, *The Smugglers.*

Greer Enterprises, which owned the El Paseo, and car dealer turned theatre owner Don Beers were in fierce competition over the years, but

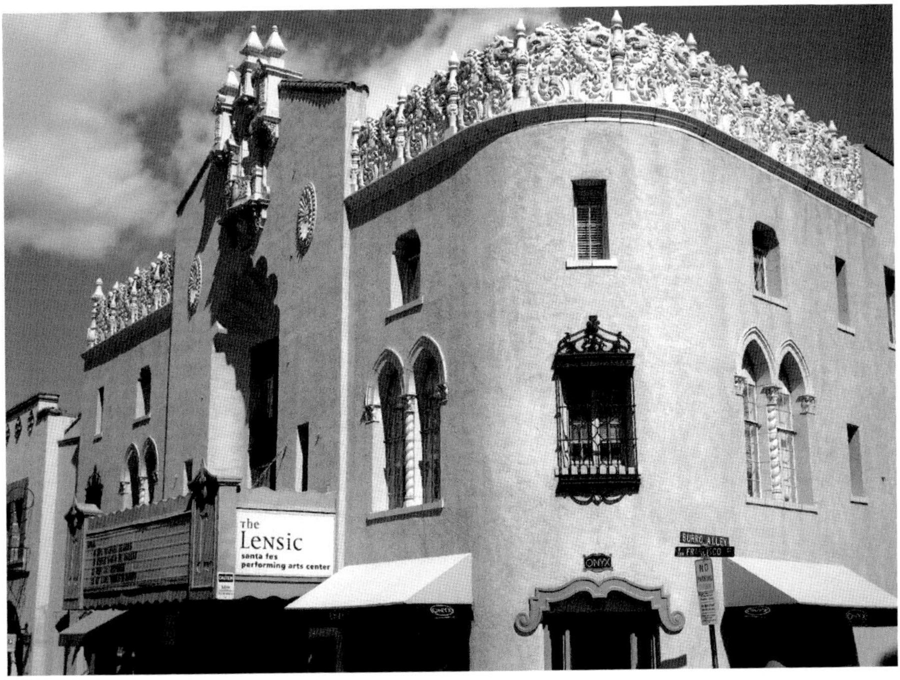

Lensic Theater, 2017, Santa Fe. *Photo by Ysabel Velarde.*

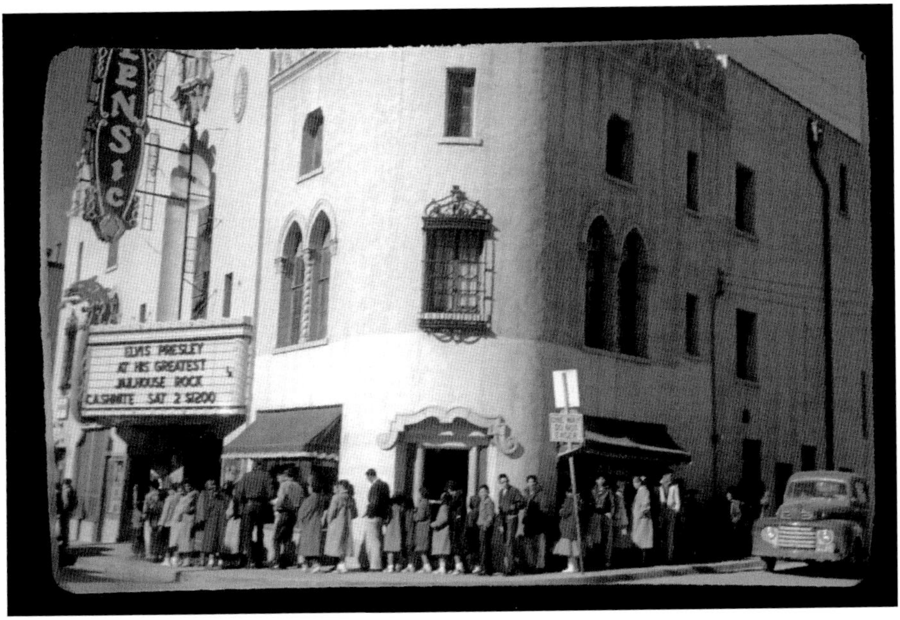

Lensic Theater, 1957. *Nichole DeWolf, personal archives.*

this became very beneficial to Santa Fe movie lovers. The Santa Fe might have had an edge by showing more cartoons for the little folks and offering free holiday matinees and prizes for the small fry. Beers's enterprise was sold in 1957.

Greer kept going, however, and opened one of the city's first drive-ins, the Pueblo. The Pueblo was located north of the village of Tesuque, which is about five miles from Santa Fe. It hosted four hundred cars and opened in June 1950 in grand style, showing the John Ford masterpiece *She Wore a Yellow Ribbon*, with John Wayne. It cost $100,000 for Greer to open the facility. The back of the screen featured a hand-painted mural by Dine artist Quincy Tahoma featuring a warrior whose horse is scared by a passing skunk.

Sadly, and startlingly, the theatre was torn down in 1955 and relocated in Santa Fe. Speculation being what it is, this might have occurred due to the Yucca Drive-In, opened in 1948, being closer to the city and having more business. It could shelter five hundred cars and was open until Halloween 1994. The new version of the Pueblo lasted until 1985 and was demolished to make way for still another Walmart.

Today, the Screen, the Cinematheque at the Center for Contemporary Arts and the Jean Cocteau all stand by themselves, with the latter having an interesting history. It was purchased and remodeled by author George R.R. Martin in 2013, opening in 2014, with myself as assistant manager. That job ended long ago; the theatre struggles somewhat, but it is a nice auditorium that is trying hard.

The Jean Cocteau Cinema was first known as the Collective Fantasy Cinema, and it opened in June 1976. Lynne Cohen, Rich Szanyi, Anne Lewis and Mary Hetler had opened and operated the theatre on a shoestring. Then, Brent Kliewer, who was the programmer for the Collective Fantasy and now programs for the Screen from his home in Oklahoma, purchased the theatre in 1983 and retitled it the Jean Cocteau in homage to the late French filmmaker and artist. The Blue Pearl Corporation, which owned several other New Mexico screens, bought it from Kliewer in 1986. He completely redesigned the theatre, giving it a graceful and sweeping look for its 128 seats.

The Trans-Lux Corporation purchased the venue in 1989, while also having a few other operations in the state. Later, when business dwindled, it started offering a lunch menu with a free old film, something that I took advantage of at every opportunity, though many others did not. The Jean Cocteau played only arthouse-type motion pictures, but it closed in April 2006.

Good fortune smiled on the JCC, as the State of New Mexico soon leased the second-floor offices of the building with plans to reopen the cinema itself as part of the state film office, using part of the lobby for a film museum to honor some of the more than eight hundred films, television shows and movies, continuing series (at least an hour in length) and silent films that have been shot at least in part in New Mexico. However, true to New Mexico government style, the funding for that never appeared, except for an exorbitant salary for the "director" of the museum. A story by Robert Nott of the *Santa Fe New Mexican* described the ludicrous situation in fine detail in 2010:

> *A museum that never had programming or operating funds but nonetheless always found money to pay its directors—none of whom had any experience in movies or museums—is about to close.*
>
> *The Governor's Office announced Friday that the New Mexico Film Museum, housed in the former Jean Cocteau Cinema on Montezuma Avenue, would close June 30 as "a budget-saving measure."*
>
> *"It's a prudent action given the economic situation of the state right now," said Stuart Ashman, secretary of the Department of Cultural Affairs, which runs the museum. "We don't have any funding effective July 1, and this will save us the lease, the cost of the director, any maintenance on the building, etc."*
>
> *The museum was known less for fulfilling its boast to spotlight the history of New Mexico filmmaking and more for the array of governor-appointed directors who came and went.*
>
> *The museum was founded in 2003 with $100,000 from the Legislature. Ymelda DeVargas, who previously worked as an unpaid lobbyist for former Sen. Shannon Robinson, was the first director. Though a board of directors was quickly assembled, the museum announced that it would need to raise $5 million to $10 million before it could officially open.*
>
> *In 2005, the legislature approved $50,000 for renovation of the Jean Cocteau Theater as the site of the museum. Jon Hendry, then the marketing director for the state's Tourism Department* [before he resigned amid accusations of conflict of interest], *helped spearhead the museum. Hendry* [still] *is currently business agent of IATSE 480, the local film technicians' union.*
>
> *DeVargas was then replaced by India Hatch, who previously ran the New Mexico Racing Commission. Meanwhile, the board of directors disbanded.*

> *After the Jean Cocteau officially closed in the spring of 2006, the Department of Cultural Affairs, which took over the film museum that year, announced it was moving the museum into the theatre. Late in 2006, the museum screened the 30-minute public-affairs documentary* Inside Bill Richardson *at the museum. It was one of the few actual events to take place in the then-3-year-old museum.*
>
> *Early in 2007, the governor appointed former Secretary of State Rebecca Vigil-Giron to replace Hatch as director of the museum. Like her predecessors, she had no relevant experience, but boasted, "I watch a lot of movies. What more do you need?"*
>
> *Within a month, her appointment was put on hold as the state conducted an audit of her previous department, in a case involving millions of dollars in federal election funds. Hatch was called back to cover at the museum. (Vigil-Giron is still facing criminal charges involving alleged money laundering and fraud.)*
>
> *Both Hatch and her successor, Sharon Maloof, another transfer from the state Tourism Department, who took over in April 2009, earned more than $80,000 a year. In addition, Ashman said Friday, the Department of Cultural Affairs paid about $74,000 a year, including utilities and rent.*
>
> *Maloof refused to comment, later took a salary cut to a mere 55k and then retired.*

While all this hanky-panky was going on (the Maloof family were hearty contributors to Governor Richardson), the Jean Cocteau was still owned by Trans-Lux. It was vacant until early 2013, when Martin bought it, upgraded it and reopened it in August 2014.

Another arthouse theatre that opened in 1975 was the Bijou, which in 1977 became City Lights.

There were a lot of things said and written about the history of Santa Fe theatres when the Jean Cocteau opened, including the following by Bill Hill, a former owner of City Lights and later of the El Paseo in downtown Santa Fe. In an op-ed in the *Santa Fe New Mexican* in 2013, Hill wrote about the history of the theatre:

> *There has been a little movie-house history going around since the announcement of the reopening of the Jean Cocteau theater, so I thought I might add a little detail from my perspective to maybe help enrich the history that has already been stated.*

We bought City Lights Cinema, in the old Bonanza Plaza, in 1978 from a serious film student at The University of New Mexico who had been showing eclectic film classics. Collective Fantasy and City Lights were both 16mm houses at the time, meaning we had to wait a year after a film's initial release for it to be available on 16mm. This was in the days before VHS or DVD.

Within six months, we installed 35mm projectors at City Lights and we were able to offer first-run foreign and art films on day and date (current releases) of their national release, dramatically changing the movie scene in Santa Fe. The Collective Fantasy couldn't keep up, and a once-good working relationship with them soured.

We initiated a "Stay Out Late" program and showed midnight shows such as The Rocky Horror Picture Show *and* Eraserhead.

We had a Family Matinee Series every weekend showing film classics along with cartoons and Republic Serial chapters, all on 35mm.

We were the first to offer a different type of concession—espresso and cappuccino, flavored popcorn, homemade tamales, fresh fruit and fresh baked goods [thus the birth of the Chocolate Maven Bakery]. *The success of City Lights led us to the opening of the El Paseo Theatre & Cafe on San Francisco Street.*

The folks who owned the Collective Fantasy sold to Brent Kliewer, who installed 35mm, changed the name to the Jean Cocteau, remodeled, and began to sell similar items in his concession lobby/lounge. At that point, we had serious competition for the first time. The film distributors loved it, but so did the movie-going public.

In box office sales, City Lights Cinema consistently out grossed the Collective Fantasy and the Jean Cocteau.

Long story short, it out grossed the El Paseo, too. We closed it down and eventually sold City Lights to Brent.

So, for my two cents, I see City Lights Cinema as the premier movie theater in the days of old and wanted to give that funky old theater a little what's due.

The Arco Theatre, housed in a Quonset hut, had a brief history in Santa Fe before being demolished. Its 684 seats were often filled with happy-go-lucky moviegoers from sometime in October 1948 until November 1951. Its first offering was *The Homestretch*, with Maureen O'Hara and Cornell Wilde, who'd make New Mexico movie fame some years later when he starred in the made-for-TV epic *Gargoyles*, filmed in and near Carlsbad Caverns.

The Burro Alley Theater opened in September 1939 and ended its run of films (starting in 1950), many of them in Spanish, in 1968. It was gutted and made into several small shops, located across from the Lensic Theater. It had a "whimsical" burro on the top of its marquee. It is hard to say how many folks it could hold, with reports saying 550, 600 or 700. It also, on occasion, hosted spiritualist Edna Ballard for readings interpreting the I AM school of philosophy. I AM was founded by Ballard's husband and was a bit of a religious sect.

In 1971, Commonwealth Theaters operated several theatres in Santa Fe and opened the Coronado Twin in the southeast part of Santa Fe. It was state of the art for the times and was later sold, closing for good in March 1990. Ironically, its first screening was of *LeMans*, starring Steve McQueen, on a double bill with *Love Story*, which starred New Mexico resident Ali MacGraw. They later met on the set of another movie made in New Mexico, *Convoy*, became involved and got married in 1973, divorcing in '78.

Another downtown Santa Fe movie lover's paradise was the short-lived El Onate, which received high grades for its Spanish/Pueblo Revival architecture, said to be inspired by the Acoma Pueblo Mission Church. It closed within five years following a "business dispute" between Nathan Salmon and the operators of other Santa Fe picture shows.

United Artists Cinemas entered the Santa Fe market with the six-screen United Artists North in July 1991. Later sold to Regal, one of two chains that remain in Santa Fe, it became a very popular second-run house but closed in December 2011. The auditoriums could host nearly 1,800.

R. Pierce on Cinema Treasures shared this information about the UA South:

> *When Commonwealth Theatres opened the Cinema Six on July 31, 1985, it was a milestone for Santa Fe. According to the Santa Fe New Mexican, it not only doubled the number of screens in town, but now Santa Fe would be able to get the new releases at the same time as Albuquerque and Dallas. The capacity of the 864-seat theatre was 273 seats in the largest auditorium and 92 in the smallest.*
>
> *In 1985 Commonwealth Theatres was the sixth largest chain in the United States, with four locations in Albuquerque. In November of 1988, Commonwealth sold their theatres to United Artists and the local theatres were listed under the banner UA/Commonwealth. In July of 1991, the six-screen United Artists North opened at the mall and the Cinema Six, after a remodel, became the United Artists South.*

In 2002, United Artists Theatres was folded into Regal Entertainment Group. According to the New Mexican, United Artists South closed on January 7, 2007 in preparation for the new Regal Cinema in Plaza San Isidro, which opened on April 16, 2007.

The DeVargas Regal Cinema 6, which was a six-screen mall-based theatre, closed suddenly in early 2017. It probably opened as a two-screener in 1974, was sold several times and then expanded. Owned at its demise by Regal, it was the last auditorium of the huge conglomerate to go digital, not doing so until 2014. It screened mostly arthouse fare along with foreign films and strong documentaries. Lousy popcorn or not, it is missed.

There's not a lot of detail on the next theatre, other than the fact that it had more names than any theatre in the state of New Mexico. Apparently, it started its lifespan in 1974 as one of the Jerry Lewis theatres that we visited earlier. It might have also been the St. Michael's Theatre, the Capital, the Pickford and the Grand Illusion (owned by Trans-Lux) and finally got run into the ground by poor management during its time as the ahead of its time Cinemacafe.

The Cinemacafe was the first theatre in the City Different to offer a full menu of food along with comfy couches and love seats to go along with the screenings of lesser-known films and documentaries. It went bankrupt, and the building has been vacant for some years now. There is little information about the previous incarnations of this spot, sorry to say.

Santa Fe might have also had its own X-rated theatre, Art Cinema X, but information is as scarce as patrons were for this place. There is another piece of information floating around listing someone called Crazy Karen, who was perhaps crazy enough to run an adults-only theatre in 1971, but if you know about these places, do let me know.

FIN

It's been a long, sometimes strange trip, but we are now back home, blurry-eyed and sore-bottomed, but I think the journey was worth it. We covered many of the movie theatres that entertained audiences over the years, and at times, it has been sad to think that so many of the movie palaces are gone, replaced by soulless boxes, often offering movies, not films.

The difference to me between movies and films is a big one. I see movies as works that are strictly for escapism or made for the thundering hordes. The recent spate of superhero movies, mingled with computer and digital enhancement, has taken a lot of the glory and joy from the art and craft of making films. Films, on the other hand, offer strong or original stories, little CGI (computer-generated imagery) and real performances from a well-written script.

So, I hope to see you at a film someday—or, maybe when I just need a break, at the movies. Your treat.

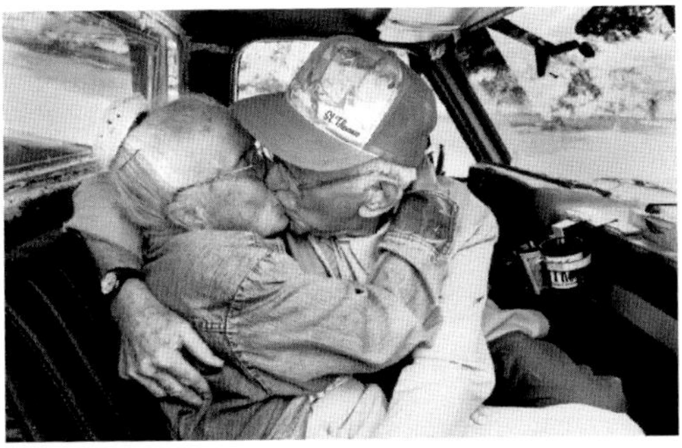

Movie? What movie? This is the best thing about going to a drive-in. *From edhat.com.*

SELECTED BIBLIOGRAPHY

CinemaTour. cinematour.com.

Cinema Treasures. cinematreasures.org.

Drive-In Theater. driveintheater.com.

Drive-In Theater Showtimes, History, Photos and More. drive-ins.com.

Film Daily Yearbook of Motion Pictures. Various years.

Harris, Jim. Interviews with the author, 2016–17.

Internet Archive. archive.org.

KRTN Radio archive. http://krtnradio.com/archive.

Lensic Theater. Lensic.org.

Melendez, Gabriel. *Hidden Chicano Cinema.* New Brunswick, NJ: Rutgers University Press, 2013.

Movie Theatres and Drive-Ins Historical Site. movie-theatre.org.

New Mexico Historic Preservation Division. nmhistoricpreservation.org.

New Mexico MainStreet. nmmainstreet.org.

New Mexico Music Commission. newmexicomusic.org.

New Mexico Music Directory. http://www.newmexicomusic.org/directory.

Newspapers.com.

Off the Road in New Mexico. offtheroadnm.org.

Pappas, Mikel Raton. *History and More.* N.p.: Coda Publications, 2003.

Robert Patrick's Personal Blog. robertpatrickpersonal.wordpress.com.

Roswell Daily Record. August 20, 2016.

Roswell Record. January 1906.

Santa Fe New Mexican. May 21, 2010; May 20, 2013; May 1, 2015.
Theatre Historical Society of America. historictheatres.org.
USDI National Park Service—National Parks Gallery.

INDEX

R

S

T

U

ABOUT THE AUTHOR

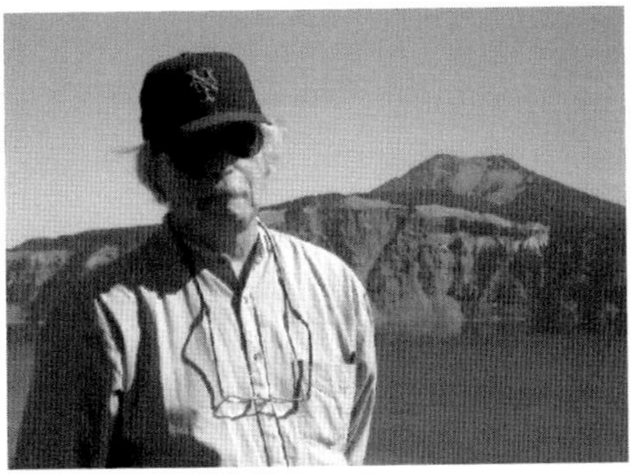

Jeff Berg remains a paradox. He resides in Santa Fe, New Mexico, where he does freelance writing and film reviews and works at the Santa Fe Humane Society as an adoptions counselor (also known as a "used cat and dog salesperson"), as well as works for the U.S. Postal Service in Tesuque, New Mexico, just north of Santa Fe. Previously, he was a board member, special events coordinator and film series programmer for the Mesilla Valley Film Society in Mesilla, New Mexico. He also worked at George R.R. Martin's Jean Cocteau Cinema as an assistant manager. His work has been featured in numerous publications, including *Film Comment*, *True West*, *New Mexico Magazine* and *ABQ the Magazine*. This is his second work for The History Press, the first being *New Mexico Filmmaking*, published in November 2015.